EVER PRESENT COMMUNICATOR

Engaging with a Dynamic God

Casper J. van Tonder

May God Bless you

Casper van Tonder

Ever Present Communicator

ISBN 978-0-9862868-7-2

ACKNOWLEDGEMENT

This project would never have been completed without the selfless and unyielding support of my wife, Vita. Thank you for your companionship and spiritual affirmation in our journey of discovery. I am forever grateful that you were willing to share some of our most precious moments in honor of the Father.

To my immediate family, I sincerely appreciate the time and effort you contributed in helping to edit this book from thousands of miles away.

A special thanks to my friends for godly support and reviewing the contents.

Most importantly, with awe and astonishment, I thank our Father in Heaven for the privilege to execute this assignment. I thank the Lord Jesus Christ for setting me free and allowing me access to the Almighty. I thank the Holy Spirit for His guidance and faithful companionship.

— CASPER VAN TONDER

CONTENTS

Such is the confidence that we have through Christ toward God. Not that we are sufficient in ourselves to claim anything as coming from us, but our sufficiency is from God, who has made us sufficient to be ministers of a new covenant, not of the letter but of the Spirit.

— 2 Corinthians 3:4-6

INTRODUCTION

We live in a time when our mind, will and emotions are under a relentless, dynamic and multi-faceted assault. The purpose of the assault is to entrap and force us to live within self-imposed limitations, strengthened by the set parameters of society. We are gently nudged from our core beliefs to a paradigm absent of absolutes. The destination is a deceptive construct where there is no defeat and no victory, only a senseless malaise of 'accepted' discontentment. This artificial environment which is bound by relativity can be manipulated by external forces at will, while we believe that we never moved an inch.

Much of the battle is focused on beating the subject into submission through exhaustion, leading to apathy and compliance. We often lose this battle too easily.

How can we possibly overcome this ever evolving matrix of deception? The only way to maintain course and live a life characterized by purpose, victory and abundance instead of mere existence, is to counter the assault with an equal or greater force.

There is such a force, such a person we can call on – God Almighty.

In a world filled with technology and information that is conveniently manipulated with the aim to supersede God, He is only reinforced. His reach and majesty extends even further than previous generations could imagine. We are able to observe God in ways that breach the traditional separation between the spiritual and natural.

God is sovereign but He does not force His will and His ways on any person. To access the reservoir of His power in your life, one has to establish a channel of communication with God that is capable of interfacing with the dynamics of His plans, purposes and methods; a channel of communication that allows you to adjust at any given moment, depending on God's guidance.

Even though the outcome with God is certain if we persist, the journey is not. Failure at junctures is inevitable and so are adjustments to the plan in order to overcome setbacks ensuring that they are short-lived and not lasting.

Since the beginning of time all things were designed and established by God to communicate His presence. Every part of creation is sustained by the dynamic power of God. Nothing is beyond the reach of His sustenance and intervention.

In the first chapter of Genesis, God announced His majesty by declaring the extent of His design and capability. God created the sun, moon, stars and planets in the universe – a spectacular masterpiece that humankind has marveled at and even worshiped for thousands of years. We are unable to expand our thoughts to truly grasp God's splendor even in this technological age. His reflection is painted on a dynamic canvas that is ever changing and growing, stretching beyond light years.

Within this paradigm of overwhelming elements of distance, time and mass, God declares that He has purposed the heavens also to communicate to mankind; His galactic billboard to announce major events.

In the book of Acts in the New Testament God reveals His resolve to communicate not only through the heavens, but also the elements present on earth. Through His Word, God declared His intent and desire to communicate with His creation.

After God created the first man Adam, the Father communed with him, taking walks with Adam in the Garden of Eden. They talked.

Throughout the Old Testament God engaged with specific individuals through angels, prophets, signs, wonders and dreams. Moses encountered God through the burning bush and the wind on the mountain, Gideon received a sign through a fleece, Joseph and Daniel had prominent dream experiences, Jeremiah and Elijah were mighty prophets of God sensitive to His Spirit. God communicated in many different ways to His servants who also acted as mediators for the nation of Israel.

The Father sent His son, Jesus Christ, to earth in the flesh. His purpose was to communicate the will of God and the secrets of His Kingdom in person. Above all Jesus communicated through His deeds.

After Jesus' death and resurrection the Holy Spirit was poured out on the disciples to empower and guide them to spread the Gospel and transform the world. The Holy Spirit was made available to every believer, allowing intimate engagement with God once again.

This book is written as a testimony to God's power, grace and mercy. The specific purpose is to practically illustrate that God constantly communicates with all who seek Him, utilizing many different methods including today's systems and technology. God's ever present desire to communicate enables mankind to have an intimate relationship with Him, but also to frequently receive practical guidance.

Spiritual principles are often relayed clearly but with little practical application. Believers, especially analytical people, are left with book knowledge. They lack the know-how to translate the knowledge into practical application that result in the release of God's power. I for one struggled to connect the dots.

Throughout the pages of this book I share my personal journey of discovery from knowledge of the Word to knowing the God behind the Word. It is a detailed account with practical examples of how my wife and I developed and learned to effectively communicate with God and allow Him to work in and through our lives, also extending into the secular world.

I am determined to continuously improve my relationship with God. My pursuit has led me to capture the wisdom gained from our encounters and translate it into a repeatable process, in order to best position myself for dynamic interaction with Him. It serves as a daily reminder of what is possible when God is involved in the situations in my life and to stay on course. We forget so easily.

It is critical in the time that we live in, to walk in the inheritance of the children of God, which comprises not only of salvation but also include the power and provision of His Kingdom. Provision that includes wisdom and support to navigate the minefield that Satan places in our paths.

Failures and 'unanswered prayers' cause many to forgo their faith and reject God. A dynamic level of communication with God allows me to continue to move forward because I know God cares and is unfailing. The fact that some of my desires have not come to pass is absorbed by the awareness of God's intimate involvement in my life in so many other areas. Communication with God builds robust trust.

This book is not a theological dissertation; it is a narrative of real life spiritual revelation through trust, risk and action leading to intimacy. My prayer is that the pages of this book will bring glory to God and fill you with the confidence to experience a close relationship with the Father. I trust that it will make you aware of the extensive spectrum of His communication methods and guide you to practically respond to His voice.

God is right here next to you and He wants to communicate with you. Prepare to expect and rise up once again in the belief that you can rely on a divine support system that is powerful and abundant.

The voice of the Lord is powerful; the voice of the Lord is full of majesty. The voice of the Lord breaks the cedars; the Lord breaks the cedars of Lebanon. He makes Lebanon to skip like a calf, and Sirion like a young wild ox. The voice of the Lord flashes forth flames of fire. The voice of the Lord shakes the wilderness;

— Psalm 29:4-9

1

TWENTY SEVEN

Confronted by the precision and fidelity of the engagement, I instinctively reached out, "Lord, is this you? It certainly appears that you are involved..." There was a sudden up shift in the rhythm of my heartbeat, filled with excitement. Awe and amazement battled with the fear of disappointment and possibly duty, to claim ownership of the sum total of my thoughts and emotions.

> You have said, "Seek my face. My heart says to you, "Your face, Lord, do I seek."
>
> — Psalm 27:8

My mind raced back to my hometown of Houston Texas, four days prior to this long awaited visit to our dear friends that now lived in California. I sat in a booth of a well-known burger chain restaurant over lunch, as I escaped the office and the frenzied rat race for a moment. My body was still in Houston, but my mind and my soul were already on the plane to Los Angeles for a break and good company that could not come soon enough.

I stared aimlessly at the receipt in my hand, my eyes focused on the order number, printed in large bold letters on an oversized slip of paper that detailed the expected special offers and survey requests. Order number "27"; time of order placed, "12:27 p.m." Deep in my spirit I knew God was communicating with me; the number would be significant. I did not know what the Lord's purpose was, but I needed to hone my senses and observe carefully in the days to follow.

With the cool California air dispersing the warmth from the sun on my back, my thoughts returned to the present as I descended from my bicycle. I am confronted with the painted house number "27...", right in front of me on the edge of the road. "This is pure coincidence; you should not get ahead of yourself. By the way, you have not been at the top of your game spiritually lately", occupied my thoughts as my soul pushed back. The conversational voices of my wife and our friends were muddled into a faint droning in the background while I moved my bicycle off the road and placed it against the fence.

In front of me was a beautiful house on the edge of a waterway that extended all the way from the ocean and meandered into the suburbs, providing easy access to the residents for boats and other watercraft. The neighborhood was mature with large palm trees and a wonderful backdrop to the mountains on the one side, and the ocean in the distance on the other side.

We had just completed one leg of a wonderful bicycle ride along the beach trail and then continued inland for a few hundred yards along the suburban roads with a specific purpose. Our friend wanted to show us this beautiful house and possibly introduce us to the people living there. As it turned out, only the children were home. Some pleasant conversation followed getting to know them and finding out what they were up to. After we said our goodbyes, we headed out to the front gate.

There appeared to be no significance to the pit-stop on our bicycle ride after all. On the way out, my eyes were drawn to the window of a side door leading to the garage. It was covered with stickers of various different organizations including charities and Christian groups. "They must be a conservative Christian family, like our friends", I thought to myself. Probing my friend, he explained that the husband owns a Christian publishing company.

So there we were, in California, at the house of what turned out to be a Christian publisher, house number "27...." My spiritual Richter Scale spiked off the chart, just after I allowed myself to relax with relief.

Five months earlier I attended a conference between Christmas and New Year. A call from the local spiritual leader went forth to all who had a testimony about the works, power and intimacy of the living God demonstrated in their lives, to write about it. To, "get the word out", because there are multitudes that still have not heard this message even with the abundance of spiritual material out there. The need far outweighs the supply. Besides, God is personal and He often handpicks the message for the recipient.

I felt in my spirit that I needed to be obedient to the call. Determined and inspired, I responded in my heart that I would do it. I would heed the call. This new found confidence was immediately tested as I heard the voice of the Lord speaking almost audibly in my heart and mind, "Don't say you will if you are not going to do it, rather say nothing. I will love you the same. Are you willing to follow wherever I lead you?" My response was,

"If I know it is you Lord, I will."

In the months that followed between that day at the conference and our trip to California, I did make an effort to translate my journey into words but never progressed further than a paragraph or two. I found myself suffocated by the worries of this world, while the Words of the Lord and my commitment faded.

Confronted by God again I knew, with little doubt, that I heard correctly the first time and that God was serious. He took me at my word that day and He was reminding me that I needed to make a choice and get on with it. Would I be obedient? He spoke to me clearly in the manner I asked Him to, simple and straight forward the way an engineer would understand, through the number *"twenty seven"* - twice.

On the way back cycling along the beach, I waited with my friend at a pier for the rest of the party to catch up. I did not share anything about my encounter and thought about what I just experienced. "Lord, thank you for clearly communicating to me in this way. You are everywhere", I prayed in my mind while I turned around to look out over the ocean. Right in the middle of the scene was a lifeguard shelter. On the side-wall it had a big number *seven* painted on it. What more did I need? Part of me felt the Lord was now just showing off. It was one of those moments where you are not sure if you should be exhilarated or quaking in your boots.

Once again several months went by after our trip to California. A chain of events was set in motion that day nevertheless. During this time God ensured that I was equipped and that the timing was right, as the desire in my heart grew to complete His mission.

I resigned from my position as America's Engineering Excellence Leader for my division at an admired multinational corporation. It would allow me to focus on completing my assignment, and I believe, adjust the direction of my life.

I was a top student in my Electrical Engineering class at university and spent fifteen years building a successful career. I climbed the corporate ladder with hard work and without stepping on others, a fact that I am proud of. Finally I was in a position where I could see myself remaining for a number of years and where I felt that I could make a significant contribution.

God blessed me with His favor. I was propelled forward in my career at certain points through God's grace when I fulfilled positions of responsibility beyond my years that required no small amount of faith to stay afloat.

I had arrived at my career goal, and the Lord responded with, "Now is the time I am asking you to focus on my assignment — it is your choice."

Many would think I am crazy. You may too. I would have agreed a few years ago. There are others that did crazy things like this too, and I am not a unique person. The journey each one of us travels though is unique.

My childhood and early adulthood were influenced by a believing, conservative church environment, with a solid foundation in the Word. I never grasped however, that there was the possibility of an 'intimate relationship with the Lord' and the reality of the works of the Holy Spirit.

My journey involves an introvert and engineer by discipline, with an analytical brain that employs reason honed by math and science. More importantly it is about a God that broke down the barriers of separation in pursuit of His beloved, to show Himself as an ever present communicator.

Nothing instills more hope than when you realize that you have been engaged by the uncontainable, unstoppable, all-powerful and infinitely intimate Creator of the universe.

The secular world and many religious participants scoff at the very notion of a God that speaks to 'ordinary' people personally, answers prayer personally and perform miracles according to their requests framed by His will. If you dare to claim this fact you are declared mentally ill, ignorant, or both by many in the liberal and conservative secular stream. A cultural stream, that is partial to the perks of a God that offers salvation but not to His Lordship. This is true regardless of the fact that the Bible is filled with accounts of God communicating with His servants on a personal level.

I am not special but I can guarantee you I am not stupid. My track record in the secular world suggests that I am not mentally ill either. That being said, my achievements are worthless compared to the works that God has done in my life, through His mercy and grace. The experiences that I share to encourage you are not that of an extraordinary person. It is about an extraordinary Father that desires to engage with all His children in a practical way illustrated through my life journey.

I know there are others with similar stories to tell, greater than mine; this book is an act of obedience to God. He insists.

But the anointing that you received from him abides in you, and you have no need that anyone should teach you. But as his anointing teaches you about everything, and is true, and is no lie—just as it has taught you, abide in him.

—1 John 2:27

2

A HISTORY OF REALITY

The privileges that we enjoy as part of life in the West are not always adequately appreciated. We are presented with many opportunities of which there is no shortage, even from an early age. Knowledge is bountiful and available.

Opportunities in itself are just possibilities and require pursuit to transform into reality. In a career driven culture everything we do is ultimately aimed to prepare us for our occupation as adults. An occupation as a measure of success, for most people, translates into a career at an organization or corporation.

A lot of attention is given to the skills and knowledge required to survive within the business world and for our families to maintain social stature. Little room is left for the wisdom of life itself. The fact that all the opportunities that we have as free people are a result of Judeo-Christian principles is a mere afterthought or not thought of at all.

Knowledge and wisdom are two very different concepts.

Wisdom implies knowledge but knowledge does not imply wisdom. Wisdom transcends knowledge.

In the pursuit of even amicable personal goals, it is easy to end up knowing how to punch the buttons on the calculator to solve complex equations without having any idea of how the math is done. When the standard buttons on the calculator do not fit the problem to be solved, the operator is either lost or uses the available buttons to bring about a result that is inaccurate. The calculator in a sense controls the user, because the user is unable to use the calculator as a tool in an environment where the demands are beyond the capabilities of the calculator.

In a society where the divorce rate is fifty percent, even amongst the religious, it is clear that many succeed in their careers but not in life. Little time is available or allocated towards understanding the foundations of a robust outlook on life. The retreat from eternal principles is justified by a re-classification of noble values to diminished importance.

Even in some seminaries today, God's truth is filtered through man's knowledge based on the notion that newer is better. The truth is that new is not really new in the context of an environment of absolutes we find ourselves in. Popular culture will argue that there are no absolutes; this argument is also not new as a brief study of the major civilizations in history proves.

Newer merely means closer to utilizing the full extent of a particular part of creation that God put in place before humankind existed. It may be new to the human experience but still utilizes truths, laws of physics and information (for example DNA) that have been present for thousands of years.

Like an application running on an operating system on your computer or smart device, the program cannot change the way the operating system functions. The application runs within the environment determined by the operating system. Changes in the operating system however can impact all or a selection of programs running within its environment. Similarly, man's progressions do not alter God's absolutes, but God can certainly impact our world.

Would it not be helpful to understand the operating system or at least where to access the properties that impacts the application that you are using? Or even better, would it not be great if you knew the programmer personally, so you can ask him to make a change in the operating system; a change that would allow your application to work or function beyond its own capabilities by utilizing the resources of the operating system ?

Throughout history, including the history recorded in the Bible, God offered men and women access to His 'operating system' and the programmer Himself. History and cyclical progression does not change the reality of God's truths, power and wisdom.

~~~~~~

Born in the seventies I grew up in a religious Christian home. We went to church most Sundays although my involvement was mostly limited to attendance only. I did no more and no less than what was expected by the general church culture in South Africa. A healthy respect for God was evident in the principles employed in our family.

Growing up as a child, there were many times when I just could not be bothered to make my way to church (conveniently located at the next corner of the street). Still, for the most part I enjoyed church. I enjoyed listening to the Bible stories, especially if the teaching of the day was from the Old Testament. Tales of how a mighty God continuously showed Himself strong by saving His people from their enemies, and how He chose and supported certain individuals to accomplish mighty feats with His help. Throughout the history of the Old Testament, God showed Himself to be slow to anger but uncompromising on His standards of godliness.

It all seemed very exciting, this dynamic relationship of an unstoppable, victorious, yet compassionate God with His people way back then. But that was the problem, it all happened 'way back then'. That was my reality.

Once I left the church services the excitement would dim - I was back in the real world. A world characterized by form and the ticking of boxes. The Bible stories lived on, but only as lessons that provide knowledge about the past and maybe to provide inspiration to do the right thing. There was no expectation to have the same relationship with God as many of the heroes of the Old Testament had.

I did enjoy the sermons on the birth of Jesus Christ and the miracles He performed, even though as a child the Old Testament stories were more appealing to me. The birth of Christ, as I understood it, was the reason why I would get to go to heaven. It was also the reason why so many in the church culture, including myself at times, chose to believe that we were set free from the responsibility to live a righteous life — a "get out of jail free" ticket.

The teaching was clear. We are saved by grace. A lot of attention was placed on keeping the law as a secondary requirement.

The application of the message was not so surgical. Most gladly received the grace teaching but not many were resolute to live according to standard set by God, especially when it was inconvenient. There was no reason to do so besides being accepted and respected by the general culture and maybe out of a feeling of guilt.

~~~~~~

The danger of grace without relationship is that it does not function as intended. It is stripped of its power. Relationship and the presence of the Holy Spirit instill a desire to please God instead of feeling obligated to please God. The desire to do something makes a huge difference in the execution of any activity.

To practice God's law in an effort to work your salvation leads to death because salvation is obtained only by accepting the Son of God. Sincere effort to keep the law out of thanksgiving for the grace of God empowers us by tempering our armor against Satan's attacks.

The Bible is clear that faith without works is dead and that speaking faith, but willfully committing habitual sin leads to rejection by God.

~~~~~~

Sermons about the death and resurrection of Jesus Christ was always a somber affair for me. The savior died. Jesus was resurrected of course and sits at the right hand of God the Father ... but ... He is in heaven and we are here alone on earth.

Apologies, I did not include the fine print. Jesus did promise the Holy Spirit would come and assist His disciples once He departed from this earth. The Holy Spirit was poured out in force to powerfully enable and guide the disciples to spread the Good News with astonishing success and reach. Then they died.

What about the Holy Spirit? As per the fine print, I understood that we should not expect much in terms of miracles or the dynamic and interactive relationship with the Executive arm of the Trinity in our lives today.

~~~~~~

There are churches that teach as a specific doctrine that the gifts of the Holy Spirit have ceased and are only applicable to Biblical times. The companionship, comfort and support of the tangible power of God on earth, were now downsized and limited to a role of implementing the sovereign will of God by exception. God does monitor and help us carry our burdens from afar, but we are left to our own devices with the ability only to live a natural life of working, maybe raising a family and then departing this world. Our faith is reserved only for enabling our own salvation.

If the gifts and close interaction with the Holy Spirit did cease, it implies that so did the great commission of sharing the Gospel with all of mankind. Our purpose then in life is to basically hang on until the day we die and go to heaven. This belief cannot be justified without qualifying that salvation is by osmoses, and that as a believer you have no responsibility towards the salvation of another. Or stated more directly, that you deserve salvation and others don't.

To a large extent believers have moved from expanding the Kingdom of God and the great commission to self-preservation. Society dictates that any normal person should expect no more, in stark contrast to the Word of God.

> So also faith by itself, if it does not have works, is dead.
>
> — James 2:17

The enemy we face every day is extremely skilled, determined and focused. He most often comes to us in the form of an acceptable compromise with legitimate reason and backed by selective theology. His objective: to lull God's people into a false sense of security, complacency and contentment. He wants mankind to roll ourselves into a blanket of religion where Satan and hell have been unofficially relegated to superstition and church is what one does on Sundays.

In this belief system, to avoid defeat by not fighting at all, rather than fighting to win, is portrayed as wisdom because nobody gets hurt. Not fighting is defeat. Many in the religious culture have fallen and continue to fall into this trap, and insist that relevance to modern society is more important than teaching the Gospel truth. Not only is this a state of deception but it is a source of deception to those who have no understanding of God. It is more dangerous to think you are right with God than not to believe in God at all. At least when you don't believe in God you may be open to hear about salvation.

There are many Spirit-filled churches that move with power, attended by those who sincerely seek the truth rather than to be 'right'. Many brothers and sisters in Christ however are still ineffective as spiritual individuals. Many have settled for a proxy faith that depends on the pastor, minister, evangelist or other leader's anointing from God.

This is Satan's 'Plan B' underpinned by two accusations:

- You are not worthy.
- God interacts in ways that you don't understand by yourself and never will.

These accusations effectively trim the Christian army down to a few soldiers and a magnitude of helpless civilians. Both of the accusations are completely false as will be illustrated through my experiences with God.

~~~~~~

As I matured during my High School years, as much as a teenager can, the teachings of the New Testament did touch my heart and inspired me to live a good life. It made good sense and did align with who I wanted to be. I did have great respect for the Father and the Son, but I cannot proclaim that I truly loved the Lord at the time. I cared about Him but I would describe it as respect rather than love.

Although I made mistakes, there were people around that were way worse than I was - in fact not even in the same ballpark. Therefore, I deserved at least some share in being selected to go to heaven. It also justified ignoring, rather than reaching out to those who were not living the 'good life'. I was picked and they were not and that was their problem.

I had no reference framework to question that belief. Maybe I wasn't a bad person but I sure was spiritually selfish. I worked hard at school, excelled academically in all subjects, with math, science and languages my top subjects. Rugby was my favorite sport and I played for the high school senior team but I wasn't the typical football player. Introverted, quiet and somewhat removed from the girlfriend scene, I enjoyed the company of my pals.

During my final year of high school it was time to decide what career path I would follow. At the time I really did not have a clue what I wanted to do. My father was an engineer and my brother who is five years older than me pursued the same occupation. Who was I to buck the trend? So I set out to become an engineer.

Even though I met the academic requirements, I found out quickly during scholarship interviews that in the real world much more emphasis was put on your other skills.

I did not sell myself very well. The pressure started to mount, but God blessed me with a scholarship to study Electrical Engineering sponsored by the country's Electricity Supply Commission.

The person who interviewed me liked the fact that I was reserved and calm. This is funny, because one of my work colleagues recently remarked that I am very intense and purpose driven. Once you encounter God in a dynamic bidirectional relationship it is hard to be reserved and calm.

I do not imply that you don't have peace and rest in the Lord. However, the fact that the almighty God takes time to listen and talk to a mere human being, demands the pursuit of excellence in everything that is worthwhile doing.

The four years of my degree course were bitter sweet. It was definitely one of the best periods in my life. I loved the freedom, the social scene and all the great young people I met. Electrical Engineering, I found out, was one of the most difficult and work intensive courses you could take. I spent many nights in my room with my fellow engineering discipline students studying for test weeks and exams while most of the student community was partying. Many an engineer that attempted that lifestyle ended up completing the course in six years or more. The upside is it really inspires your prayer life.

I was involved in the major student church located on campus, the predominant church denomination within the culture. Most Christians that I was aware of, were born, raised and buried within the same church denomination.

Some of my best experiences and memories were formed taking part in church initiatives during vacation times. Both a Biblical drama tour and a cycling tour were undertaken to raise funds and bring godly principles to the churches and resorts along the journey. A truly honest assessment however would reveal that part of the attraction of these initiatives was to spend time, get closer or start a relationship with that special young lady. Church events served as the gathering ground of good Christian specimens.

To say I supported these initiatives because I belonged to Christ as the primary reason would be a lie. After all, I always kept a safe distance from those over the top students who did not go to the mainstream church but chose to venture into realms of the charismatic church movement.

Society dictated that times had changed and some of the Biblical principles could not be applied to the world we live in. It was a handy excuse to disqualify any notion of spending precious time to see if there was anything to what I perceived, based on my background, as arty and needy types exercising their chaotic spiritualism.

After all, we were a community of intelligent students that were taught reason and logic that helped us understand all the mysteries of the world in the terms of math, physics, psychology, biology and other foundations of human wisdom.

When in trouble it is easy for you to contradict yourself. During times of high stress or heartache I often called out to the Lord looking at Him to speak to me clearly and plainly. I needed an answer 'immediately'. Because I needed it immediately, this seemed to be the logical time for God to speak.

I was asking so urgently, quoting every related Bible scripture....but there were no voices, no sign, no nothing from God. Urgency turned into anger and finally into despair. Surely, God really had stopped communicating to His people in an interactive way. It was stupid to think otherwise, I thought. I was just a number in His organization and He was far removed in His corner office up in the sky. God would not speak to a peasant like me.

This cycle of sincere urgency followed by silence and despair would repeat itself. Why? Well, there was something inside of me, however small at the time, refusing to give up on the idea that God interacting with His people was still a reality and not just Biblical history. I entered into adulthood and the business world with a solid foundation in Biblical principles and respect for God. This was not enough however to prepare me for a world outside of my chosen friendships and family. A world filled with dark forces, where more than Biblical knowledge was required to meet the challenges, stay true to my faith and not be crushed.

This was the start of a journey with God where Biblical history became reality.

For our struggle is not against flesh and blood, but against the rulers, against the authorities, against the powers of this dark world and against the spiritual forces of evil in the heavenly realms.

— Ephesians 6:12

3

PARADIGM SHIFT

Imagine yourself for a moment standing in a brightly lit room. All objects in the room are clearly visible to you. Every object that obstructs the light source can be distinguished by the shadow that it casts. You are aware of areas of the room that are obstructed from view, identified by the lack of visibility.

When the light is suddenly switched off, all visibility is lost due to the absence of light. Having been exposed to the light, your eyes are unable to see anything at all. You are well aware of the darkness, the dangers that lurk under its cover and therefore remain stationary to avoid injury to yourself.

After a while your eyes start to adjust to the darkness and your surroundings begin to look familiar again. As time passes, your eyes adjust to the darkness more and more, until the objects in the room are seen in grey scale. The room does not really seem that dark at all anymore.

Now you feel safe enough to move about in the room, confident that you would be able to see the obstacles in the way. As you walk further and further your confidence grows. Suddenly you are brought to the ground by an electrical cord on the floor acting as a trip wire; indistinguishable from the floor surface obscured by twilight.

It is with good reason that the Bible instructs us to flee from sin instead of trying to outwit it. Darkness alters the true appearance of all that is covered by its veil. We never truly know what we are up against or what dangers lurk in the dark. When we find out it may be too late. I discovered that darkness is best avoided.

~~~~~~

I always enjoyed spending time at home, even while attending university. It is a testimony to my family but also my personality. I liked and still do enjoy familiar surroundings and the company of friends and family.

The irony is that I have spent most of my life working and living abroad in an unfamiliar environment. It was a direction that in all probability I would not have chosen on my own. What we want in our limited vision and what we need from God's omnipresent perspective is sometimes very different. God does place desires in our heart that is not in conflict with His plans and purposes. Ultimately His plan for us is to have an abundant and satisfied life. At the same time God's will is for us to reach the level of spiritual maturity to live His dream, without losing ourselves in the process. We can only live in God's abundance if we are able to stay on the course that He communicates to us.

People don't like to change and typically only do so if circumstances force us to. We often get upset as I did at times. It soon became clear though that the toughest times are the most precious. During those times I had the opportunity to forge a more intimate relationship with the Heavenly Father.

After I finished my studies, I was presented with an opportunity to work on assignment at a business in Ireland, as student placement. Professionally I was excited about the opportunity as the experience would definitely further my career prospects, but on a personal level I had mixed feelings.

Most young people would jump at the opportunity but for me it was leaving my familiar environment, family and friends behind. Fortunately I had my father to guide me. My dad was a successful engineering manager at a petrochemical company. He set high professional and academic standards and was well respected by his peers. His guidance steered me to override my personal feelings and pursue a rare opportunity.

In the middle of the winter of 1998, my fiancé and I arrived in the Republic of Ireland just south of the border with Northern Ireland. It was an industrial town, which hosted many factories of global electronics based equipment manufacturers. Ireland was popular at the time due to tax benefits, reasonably priced labor and the wet climate that provided a clean air environment ideal for electronics.

We had a great time in Ireland. The people were very sociable and friendly. After a while everybody knew about the South Africans and we were frequently greeted by passing cars as we made our way on foot or bicycle. Although it was a safe place to live for foreigners there were some tension in the community. In an otherwise peaceful environment we were reminded of the underlying tensions by occasional bomb threat alerts. The struggle between the factions in Northern Ireland spilled over the border every now and then.

We were privileged to be in Ireland at the time when the Good Friday agreement was signed. The agreement was a historical event and paved the way to a more peaceful existence.

Ireland presented a dual shock to my system. It was my first professional full time employment and the first time I had to communicate in my second language English, all the time. Not to mention decoding the strong Irish accent.

The underlying friction between the Catholic and Protestant communities in the country immediately became apparent. We met a young couple of whom the guy was protestant and his girlfriend Catholic. The couple felt comfortable to tell us about their backgrounds because we were foreigners and from the younger generation. Their relationship would be frowned upon by the landlord and the landlord would have evicted them if he found out. As much as I love the Irish, the challenge was magnified by engaging with a vastly different culture from what we were used to.

I was ignorant to the complex mix of religion and politics that influenced the Irish and other societies in Europe. This was my first taste of how rulers through the ages preferred power over purity and used religion to achieve some of their goals. The impact is still felt today. The effect of culture on how Christianity is practiced was evident in South Africa, but I did not experience this intense influence from both culture and politics on faith. It was an eye opener for me and also made me wonder how much my own faith was influenced by culture.

Similar to many countries in Europe, the general population did not attend church on a regular basis. There were many beautiful churches and cathedrals but few faithful participants.

I soon found out that the words "Jesus Christ" was frequently used to curse in all walks of life. It was a very common expression in the secular world. The intensity of using the Lord's name in vain was hard to stomach even though I still had a long way to go with my relationship with God. Every time a local would use this expression I would be enraged.

How could they continuously disrespect the name of the Lord in such blatant arrogance? I was angry and rightly so but the anger was not complemented by compassion for the lost. There was a self-righteous element to it. The Holy Spirit had not yet changed my heart. As time went by I became used to this unacceptable behavior.

We were invited to a Christening service and were really looking forward to attending, only to discover that the main feature would be the drinking party that followed. As with most social events, beer was the main attraction. Drinking yourself into a stupor was a favorite pastime of many, especially of our age group.

I was raised in a home where alcohol was consumed very moderately. Even at university, besides for the odd occasion, consumption was moderate in my close circle of friends. Being a young foreigner and trying to fit into a strange culture was hard enough. Now I was continuously on the defense and confronted with the constant stream of flack because I did not drink that much.

My supervisor lived next door to the manager of the local rugby club. If I recall correctly, it was my second day of work when I got called into my manager's office. Not for work, but to present an opportunity for the boy from South Africa, where rugby is almost a religion, to come and check out the local rugby club that Sunday. I loved playing rugby, did not play regularly since I left school and jumped at the opportunity. I headed across town on my bicycle.

By some miracle it stopped raining before noon that day, for which I was very thankful. You'll understand why in a moment. My expectation was to watch the games and meet some people. This expectation was soon turned on its head.

It was half time during one of the games when the coach came walking up to me and asked whether I wanted to play. I was completely unfit and out of form, besides, it was too cold and the surface too wet for the guy still sporting some sun tanned legs from the African sun. I did not feel up to it. The only legitimate excuse that I was able to come up with was, "I don't have any kit with me."

The coach looked at me with a distant expression on his face. I did not realize he was sizing me up. The next thing I knew, he called over 'one of the lads' and instructed him to take his kit off (boots and all) and hand it over to me.

Within five minutes I was ankle deep in mud and playing my first rugby game in Ireland which felt like playing in quick sand. I distinctly remember the coach having a go at me from the sideline because I was too slow around the pitch. The nerve … I was out on my feet navigating puddles of mud and thick patches of grass.

The rugby club gave me the opportunity to travel around the country and experience the culture while having another chance at reliving my glory days of playing the game I loved. On the flip side, I was injected into a culture of heavy drinking and loose morals as seen from my perspective. I was very thankful at the time that my future wife was with me as temptation lurked around every corner.

Even though I was a dim beacon of light and shared my faith as the reason for not joining in on most occasions, I did succumb to the peer pressure a few times and consumed too much alcohol for my own good.

One night I got a rude awakening to the dangers that lurked in the shadows. Because I wasn't a seasoned drinker, even though I paced myself, the evening was just too long. I left a pub with a couple of guys from the rugby team. They had a conversation about me while standing right next to me. I assumed they thought I would not be able to follow the conversation... "He is not as strong as he thinks he is, we should take him back to the apartment and work him over", one of them said with the other nodding in agreement. Their intent was clear and wasn't honorable. They intended to force themselves on me.

The shock pretty much sobered me up. Instinctively, I fired off a call for help to the Lord and regardless of the mess I got myself into and the environment I chose to explore, He answered immediately! He met me where I was at, waiting for me to 'switch on the light.' He is ever present and His grace and mercy is incredible as He draws one into the shadow of His wings; even if most calls to His office is in case of emergencies only.

Out of nowhere, a group of people appeared on otherwise empty streets and I stealthily left the scene and made my way back home. Thankfully, they did not follow me.

Knowing their normal day to day life, I would have never suspected the violent and sexual immoral intent that had a hold of their souls. What a disappointment! I later found out that others were aware of their endeavors.

The God appointed time in Ireland exposed me to places, activities and atmospheres that brought with it awareness that there were truly dark forces at work all around us and their draw is very strong and enticing. Spiritual forces can overrule the subject that they influence dramatically. The same experiences could have been acquired back home in South Africa, but the isolation from a familiar pocket of culture, family and friends accelerated the process.

~~~~~

We are not only surrounded by people, but also by evil that disguises itself incredibly well and prides itself in remaining inconspicuous. If you are ignorant, naïve or ill equipped from a spiritual point of view you will get drawn into quicksand that is hard to escape. In fact, impossible to escape, without being honest with yourself about the true desires of your sinful nature and being fully dependent on the power of God to direct your steps. The forces of darkness are romanticized by popular culture but as human beings we are not strong enough to withstand them. They dwell within the realm of the 'operating system'.

One may think that you will never get into situations like the one I described and therefore do not need to experience the power of the Lord's protection and presence in such a way. The reality is that evil is never far away and will do all it can to make you ineffective, especially when you become aware that it is real. If we are not prepared, we get knocked down and live disillusioned, fatalistic and ineffective lives. Salt that has lost its saltiness.

> You are the salt of the earth. But if the salt loses its saltiness, how can it be made salty again? It is no longer good for anything, except to be thrown out and trampled underfoot. "You are the light of the world. A town built on a hill cannot be hidden. Neither do people light a lamp and put it under a bowl. Instead they put it on its stand, and it gives light to everyone in the house."
>
> — Matthew 5:13-16

We need the One who knows all things and sees all things to be our guide because the most dangerous traps are unseen and religion without relationship tends not to expose them but rather provide them with sanctuary.

~~~~~~

The Lord saved me that night. I became acutely aware that the unseen world is very real and dangerous. Lightly walking with the Lord is not good enough. Yet God is faithful even if we are not, as long as our hearts are repentant and long for Him.

And we know that in all things God works for the good of those who love him, who have been called according to his purpose.

— Romans 8:28

4

BEST MADE PLANS

After I returned home to South Africa, my career path and life were set out in my mind. Start my long term career, get married and support a family. God however had different plans.

Before I went to Ireland I had obtained approval from the corporation that sponsored the scholarship for my studies to delay my start date by six months. All parties agreed that the assignment and experience gained abroad would be a win-win situation.

To fulfill His purposes in molding the miry clay God makes the impossible possible. While in Ireland I received correspondence from my sponsor that they were absolving me from all work and financial obligations towards them due to a lack of positions to employ graduate students. After working for an American based global corporation in automation engineering for almost a year, a senior manager at the corporation that provided my scholarship, asked if I would return. He explained that they never intended to let me go and it was a mistake.

As it turned out God had ordained circumstances to release me from this obligation, not to fulfill my plans but to fulfill His future plans for me.

~~~~~~

Obedience that validates faith is of great importance to our Father but His grace and mercy toward us dwarfs our efforts. God's blessing is an enabler for the Kingdom of God — not a golden handshake from the Almighty. We are all equal before God. Our citizenship of the Kingdom of God is our inheritance but also our calling, two sides of the same coin.

For many religious participants in the West duty is not at the forefront anymore. It has been replaced by consumerism. Acceptance of duty releases the power and authority that comes with responsibility and obedience. Power that penetrates into the realm of the spiritual — an authority that can alter the game plan from defense to offense.

~~~~~~

Every experience in life serves as preparation for the next, and my time in Ireland served to prepare me to be bold in what I believed in, what I stood for, and the dangers of not standing tall. Not because of own pride and self-righteousness, but for the sake of the Gospel.

I enjoyed working in the Durban (South Africa) office and I had a good relationship with my colleagues. As the rookie, and by nature quiet and reserved, I sat at my desk and kept to myself most of the time. I ventured out to the construction floor on occasion to oversee the building and testing of project system cabinets, and interacting with technicians, fellow engineers and customers when required.

My boss called me in one day for a 'sit-down'. He was much like me when he was younger. He advised me that no matter how technically skilled I was, I would have to emerge from my corner and engage with people on a regular basis to progress in my career. Those words stuck with me and turned out to be very true.

The twist in the plot was that God took me and transformed me while serving Him, not the world. He gave me exactly those skills at the right time to propel my career in the secular world. Although the business reaped the benefits, the development work was done by the Master Himself in the church environment.

Generally in the world, especially a world without Christ, it is all about progression and in a very clever way people help others only to help themselves. "The generous will prosper" (Proverbs 11:25) is frequently replaced in the business world by "The prosperous will be generous"; justification to step on everybody on the way to prosperity.

It took me a long time to face this fact, as I always tried to believe the best about others. You could argue that business is business, but I had the privilege of working with great individuals that excelled despite valuing people more than money in a profit driven environment; people that served as inspiration to me.

We occasionally finished work early on a Friday afternoon to grill ("braai" in South African terms) while socializing with the team. The first time that I was involved in this, the office administrator came to me and asked if it would be in order if she got everybody the same meat, since we had guys working in the office that had specific religious requirements for the food that they ate. Nobody had a problem with this. I decided to take a stand for my faith.

The modern Western culture is often ignorant of spiritual implications as it relates to Christianity. Even if there is a true understanding of the Bible's teaching, Christians are too afraid to offend, because that means hurting others (in the short-term). This mindset surrenders to the great deception that truth is secondary to political correctness.

Very amicably I responded that I don't eat food dedicated to other religions and requested 'standard' meat for myself. My statement was greeted with a look of surprise on the administrator's face. She responded that there was nothing wrong with the meat, it was just normal meat. To which I replied, that I knew the meat is the same but as a Christian I do not believe in the way in which and to whom the meat is dedicated upon slaughter. By eating the meat, in this case where there was a choice, I would in effect deny my faith by elevating another god above my own. I would imply that my God is secondary and does not matter enough to warrant marginal inconvenience. I respected the guys being true to their religion but did not support their belief, the same as they did not support mine. My follow up statement was met with an "Oh, I see" with a blank face from the administrator.

But if anyone loves God, he is known by God. Therefore, as to the eating of food offered to idols, we know that an idol has no real existence and that "there is no God but one." "For although there may be so-called gods in heaven or on earth as indeed there are many "gods" and many "lords" yet for us there is one God, the

Father, from whom are all things and for whom we exist, and one Lord, Jesus Christ, through whom are all things and through whom we exist. However, not all possess this knowledge. But some, through former association with idols, eat food as really offered to an idol, and their conscience, being weak, is defiled. Food will not commend us to God. We are no worse off if we do not eat, and no better off if we do. But take care that this right of yours does not somehow become a stumbling block to the weak. For if anyone sees you who have knowledge eating in an idol's temple, will he not be encouraged, if his conscience is weak, to eat food offered to idols? And so by your knowledge this weak person is destroyed, the brother for whom Christ died.

— 1 Corinthians 8:8-11

The food in itself does not harm us as Christians because we are cleansed by the blood of Christ and are intended to live by the Holy Spirit. If we knowingly compromise only for the sake of political correctness (set by society) however we sin against fellow believers and God. Our freedom in grace should empower us, not dull our dedication.

For the next few days the subject never came up again until the Friday at the grill. The word must have spread through the office during the week. One of the guys engaged with me in a friendly manner and asked me what my problem was with their meat. I repeated the statement that I made earlier to the administrator and it was met with respect rather than offense. I believe we create more problems by displaying weak principles and self-discipline than being politically incorrect. Those whom we aim to please are often not impressed. Sincerity lacking truth displays a weakness of character. In this case the truth enabled mutual respect.

As part of my job I met and worked with people from many

major cultures globally. I discovered that the religious among them do not respect most Western people from a religious and cultural point of view for a simple reason: they see our main religion (Christianity) as weak. Not because it is weak but because too few who call themselves Christians actually stand up for their beliefs and even fewer live the teachings of the Bible. This reason causes many to go overboard with political correctness and instead of gaining favor, those practicing this doctrine lose the respect of those they aim to impress.

Facts are an interpretation of the truth relayed according to perspective or intent. Opinion is a further morphing of facts to adhere to an ideological belief. The Lord taught me that His hand operates in the truth of His Word, not facts or opinion regardless of the potential consequences. I needed to pursue finding the truth in all situations, not blindly but with wisdom and love.

After a year with the Durban office, my newlywed wife and I left the shores of South Africa once again for Scotland on a two year work assignment for the company.

Now the Lord is the Spirit, and where the Spirit of the Lord is, there is freedom.

— 2 Corinthians 3:17

5

A NEW BEGINNING

Our two year stay in Scotland turned into ten. God transformed our hearts, minds and understanding of the Kingdom of God during this time. Although I do not know all the details of the journey ahead, I do believe that the ten years in Scotland were spiritually the most transformative years in my own and also my wife's lives.

"You looked like rabbits staring into the headlights of a car when you arrived at Edinburgh airport", my manager would remind me every now and then in jest. This was a gentle description coming from a Scotsman. In Scotland nobody is off limits and we soon learned to laugh and have fun at our own expense. Well, actually it took a year or two!

We arrived in the late summer of 1999 and found that Scotland was a beautiful country with very sociable and passionate people. Scottish passion is well portrayed by the character of William Wallace in the block buster movie "Brave Heart."

Unfortunately, in some areas of the country there were high levels of alcohol consumption, teenage pregnancies and substance abuse. Many of the challenges experienced in these areas may have been brought on by the dreary weather featuring grey skies and rain for a very large portion of the year. The long winter nights and grey skies took some getting used to for my wife and I.

We experienced the culture as a post Christian society in general. It was not popular to be a practicing Christian and less so to be a born-again Christian. The born-again Christians were strong and dedicated. Little room was left for compromise. Compromise meant defeat in a hostile spiritual environment.

We spent the first few months adapting. The long dark nights often caused us to go to bed very early. When we first arrived we had very little money to spend. The exchange rate between the British Pound and South African Rand was one to ten at the time.

We spoiled ourselves by dining at the least expensive burger place we could find. It took ages to order food in the beginning because the attendants would have to repeat ten times what was said, for us to finally understand the accent.

Thinking we were very clever, we would eventually learn the sequence of questions by heart and then have the answers ready without knowing what was said. The sequence normally went as follows, "May I take your order? What drink do you want? Small, medium or large? Sit in or take away (carry out)?"

Our success rate turned out to be less than fifty percent as there always seemed to be some promotion or option thrown in and our whole sequence fell apart. All we could do is break out in laughter and spend the next five minutes conveying our order.

After a number of weeks we decided that it was time to find a local church family. I must confess that my wife was leading the effort. I was somewhat disabled by the pressures of work and adapting to the culture and weather. This assignment was not a six month stint as we did in Ireland. This was part of my career and I had to be successful in unfamiliar surroundings where I struggled to understand the Scottish accent, especially living close to Glasgow.

My wife would head out to look for a church on a Sunday morning and come back only to report, that all the wonderful historic churches that she entered in town were filled with about twenty people. Most of the attendees were past the age of retirement. Nobody greeted her or showed interest. Similar to Ireland, the main denominations are Protestant and Catholic. Religion and politics merge to bring separation even to the level of the two major local football teams. One supported by Protestants and the other by Catholics in general. My wife focused on the Protestant churches because of our Lutheran background.

We were in our early twenties and looking for something a little younger and alive. In time we found out that there were a few vibrant churches but we did not know where they were located. God decided to lend a helping hand and ensured that we were exposed to the church He had in mind for us.

My wife drove past a building that was located on a plot of land intended for a house, during one of her Sunday church-hunting trips. It was the size of a big house and filled the plot of land almost completely. It had a big sign outside indicating it was a "Christian Centre."

She did not quite know what that meant but there were many cars lining the street at this building. Everybody was inside though as the service had already started. My wife parked on the sidewalk, and got out of the vehicle to investigate. Right at that moment a friendly student girl who arrived late confirmed that it was indeed a church and invited her to attend right there and then.

God's detailed timing led us to our new church home in a foreign country. It did take some time to verify that this was our new home, as it turned out to be a charismatic church and we were not used to that kind of environment at all.

Up to that time we had called charismatic churches, 'happy clappy' churches. Attending the church was somewhat of a departure from our background. The town we now lived in was not very affluent. The church also was not very affluent or glamorous but there was a 'Spirit' present in those who attended; a Spirit that caused us to stay there while we were resident in Scotland.

The Holy Spirit, whom we had much to learn about, was elevated to His proper place in the lives of the church leadership and many in the congregation.

Being alone in Scotland away from family, friends and our familiar 'church paradigm', allowed us the space and freedom to explore, investigate and test the new environment unhindered. Fervent prayer by my brother and his wife for us to find a Spirit-filled church was answered. God's plan was in action.

We spent several Sundays just sitting at the back of the church observing everything. For a start the worship part of the service lasted an hour and then the sermon lasted another hour. Coming from 'sixty minutes or else' services, strictly governed by the agenda, this was quite a shock to the system. Later on we started to arrive later to miss some of the worship so we could last the duration. We did notice though that many did not mind repeating the same verses over and over to exalt and glorify God.

Speaking in tongues was practiced with subsequent interpretations. People went to the front in response to the message of the day. They committed to make a practical stand to change or receive the deliverance needed in their lives. "Do these people have no self-respect", I thought. How could the pastor expect people to expose their needs and failures like this in public? I thought this only happened behind closed doors in the pastor's office. There was recognition that "...all have sinned and fall short of the glory of God" (Romans 3:23).

Over time the Lord changed us in this environment where the Bible was the unquestionable Word of God. His Word did not stay on the pages of a 'book' but were practiced in everyday life and applied as it was written. God's Word, His ways and the gifts of the Holy Spirit were the first stop instead of the last stop to approach daily living. God's Word was alive and it carried revelation and creative power.

Attending many events where the presence of our Lord Jesus and the Holy Spirit was so evident, bred a hunger to be close to God at all the times. It was so refreshing to return to church where the worship of God's people drew His intimate presence.

Yet you are holy, enthroned on the praises of Israel.

— Psalm 22:3

We verified everything we were exposed to against the Word of God. Without interference we were set free from religion and released into relationship.

My wife and I received the baptism of the Holy Spirit. As an engineer, to get to the point of speaking in tongues took me a while! I wanted proof. I would not stand for theater or falseness to 'feel good'. I was so committed to the truth, to be honest and not to become a 'charismatic fool', that I resisted the Lord with everything in me without realizing it.

This was not a fair contest. The Lord would have to operate in spite of me. This theme was repeated many times in my life. Stubbornness probably had something to do with it. Regardless of the fact that I gnashed my teeth against the volcano welling up in my belly when the pastor was praying over me, I eventually relented and allowed the Holy Spirit to operate in this gifting also.

I thank God today that He was and is so patient with me. Only years later would I get to know how critical it is to be able to press beyond the limitations of human language and allow the Holy Spirit to communicate with the Father through you (on your behalf). Practically it means praying words that you do not understand, led by the Holy Spirit. Even though you don't understand the words, you can feel in your spirit that it is powerful and applicable to your situation. Some have the gift to interpret these words.

One of my most precious memories with the Holy Spirit was much later in my life. Family members of ours faced circumstances that seemed impossible to overcome within the required window of time. I decided to engage in prayer one night by myself. I prayed and pressed into the matter but felt powerless. Wondering about what to pray 'at' the Lord, a thought popped into my mind, "Let the Lord pray." Jesus is at the right hand of the Father, interceding for us. He lived a human life and descended to hell before He was resurrected. He understands our pain, our weaknesses and also the consequences of sin. He intercedes with a passion that we cannot even begin to imagine.

Likewise the Spirit helps us in our weakness. For we do not know what to pray for as we ought, but the Spirit himself intercedes for us, with groanings too deep for words. And he who searches hearts knows what is the mind of the Spirit, because the Spirit intercedes for the saints according to the will of God.

— Romans 8:26-27

I acted in obedience. The Holy Spirit took over and I could feel His intense presence in the room. At one point I was physically jack-knifed. I did not know exactly what the Holy Spirit was praying, but whatever it was, it had serious intent and authority directed at oppressing forces. I believe the prayer destroyed spiritual strongholds and in turn changed the natural condition.

Circumstances changed overnight that time and enabled a window of blessing that I will never forget.

As the Holy Spirit grabbed a hold of our lives a lot of things changed. We could not get enough of God. Suddenly worshipping the Lord for an hour before the message was sometimes not enough as we lost ourselves in His presence. We wanted to learn all we could, as fast as we could, to get to know God instead of knowing about God.

A discipleship course taught us what it meant to follow Jesus. It meant a renewal of the mind and heart to serve not to enforce. As this knowledge permeated our individual lives, our marriage (between two very strong but vastly different personalities), morphed into what it should have been from the beginning, oneness.

We started to serve each other instead of fighting to get what we wanted only to find that we received what we needed without having to fight for it. Fulfillment was realized by giving, not receiving. It was incredible how verses in the Bible that we read many times before, suddenly became life changing when they were

51

received and applied energized by the Holy Spirit.

Our spiritual lives changed from black and white into color.

And to him was given dominion and glory and a kingdom, that all peoples, nations, and languages should serve him; his dominion is an everlasting dominion, which shall not pass away, and his kingdom one that shall not be destroyed.

—Daniel 7:14

6

SEEK FIRST THE KINGDOM

The following is one of the most straightforward and simple, but also most powerful verses in the Bible - if you dare to apply it as it is written.

> But seek first the kingdom of God and his righteousness, and all these things will be added to you
>
> —Matthew 6:33

It conveys the core principle of obedience that so many Christians struggle with every day. Most commonly we interpret this verse to ourselves as follows, "Acknowledge God, go to church and whatever you choose to pursue with your talents will be blessed by the Lord"; especially if you are a professional person, who spent many years working hard to obtain your specialized level of education and skillset. Logic dictates that you apply those skillsets to minimize risk and maximize the chances of success.

Just as you worked hard to achieve success in the world you will also develop and maintain your righteousness through hard work and applying yourself. Right?

Wrong! The verse states," all things will be added to you." Through the lens of personal experience I would instead interpret the verse as follow, "Keep listening to find out what God wants you to do, then do whatever the Lord asks of you even though it does not align with your personal or career objectives. He will take care of the rest."

It is a constant, lifelong challenge to keep this principle in focus. Our natural instinct, particularly true pertaining to men, is to take matters into our own hands and do what we believe is required and what we are responsible for. Often we become what we do. Inherently this is not a bad trait. God designed us to provide for our families and gave us certain natural talents. The question is who or what do we serve with the talents and skills that we have?

You may argue that you do not serve anything. If you think carefully you will realize that we all serve something or somebody. Ambition, money, fame, family... As honorable as a cause may seem, if God is superseded by an earthly master, it excludes us to a large extent from experiencing the Kingdom of God at work in our lives. By seeking the Kingdom of God first, you open the door for God to intervene on your behalf and communicate guidance applicable to your daily life. God promises His help in response to obedience. One of the best and most tangible illustrations that brought this principle home happened while I was working on a project in Scotland.

~~~~~~

I became very involved in the youth ministry at our church. The youth club operated weekly on a Friday evening with intermittent special events on Saturdays and Sundays. At the same time I was very busy at work and frequently travelled to offshore oil and gas production platforms in the North Sea. Many Fridays I would land at Edinburgh airport late afternoon and drive directly to church as the meeting started around 7 p.m.

After a demanding week I often felt like skipping those evenings but found that the Lord did His best work when I had nothing left in the tank to give.

Times that I could have worked late and focused on my career but didn't, my career seemed to go smoothly and issues were either few or they just worked themselves out. When I focused on my career when I was supposed to tend to the Lord's work, my career would be hard going and issues would not get resolved.

During one of the really busy times, both at church and at work, I was placed on a project where significant problems were being experienced. Only after joining the team did I find out how far behind schedule and under pressure the project was.

From the start I did not enjoy working on this small project. As a junior engineer I felt that I was left to clean up the mess. At the same time, a planned youth club event which took up a lot of time was fast approaching. Because I had to rescue the project at work (a situation I did not create) I felt let down by God.

I grumbled at the Lord that I was trying my very best to spend time on His activities and now He allowed me to get involved with this project! The response I received from the Lord was that I would never be content while I had one foot in the world and one in the Kingdom. Basically I felt He said, "Put away the violin! I am not impressed by your sad song."

I did and got on with the job at hand. Matters on the project however deteriorated from bad to worse. We were now confronted with a customer requirement to develop a communications interface between our control system and another electronic control system. Typically this is not a big deal but in this case the data transfer was non-standard and the project did not budget for the application. There was no obvious solution, very little time and a lot of pressure to get the job done.

After some time spent on the problem I decided that if there was any chance of me getting the work done in time, or at all, I needed help. I consumed a full day phoning engineers in various locations to find out if anybody previously encountered the problem and possibly had a solution that would fit within the time and budget allocated. At the end of the day I came up with nothing.

I went back to the Lord again, this time even more wound up. I pleaded, "What is going on Lord. I am committed to your work and now you have given me this mess of a project with what seems to be an insolvable puzzle within the time constraints. I won't be able to do anything but work long hours to try and figure out a solution, not being able to engage in the ministry work. There are many eyes on me. This can impact my career. I thought you would bless the work that I do so I would have time to do Your work?"

This time my plea was met with what seemed to be silence. I thought God probably did not like my session on the soap box. But God is real and He wants us to be real too. The intent of our hearts is not hidden from Him.

The name of the production platform grabbed my attention. I was suddenly curious to find out if it had any meaning. I looked the name up using an online search engine. I thought it was probably the name of a lake or loch as they are called in Scotland.

The first search result that appeared was for a Biblical character that was known as a person that walked with God. He was regarded as a friend by God.

Finding out what the name meant in Biblical terms triggered something in my spirit that made me believe that God allowed the circumstance for a purpose. His method of communication utilized an odd name for an offshore platform to draw my interest. It strengthened my trust that the Lord would take care of the problem even if I did not know how it would happen.

My wife was surprised to find me at home early that evening. She was aware of the problems I was dealing with at work and expected that I would be home late. I decided to pack up and attend to the Lord's business as planned regardless of the problems at work.

The next day I focused on some less important activities required to complete the project, just to feel that I was making some progress. Still with no solution to the design problem, I returned to my office in the afternoon and started to organize my desk and get rid of the clutter of engineering documents and drawings that had accumulated. Some paperwork was lying on top of one of the filing cabinets. I wasn't sure if it was my colleagues' or mine, so I asked him. I was told that the paperwork was old system software logic design drawings that he had received from a customer for the project he was working on. He did not need it, because it did not relate to the scope of work that our company was contracted for.

I started to accumulate the stack of drawings to put them in the paper recycle bin. One of the drawings caught my eye as it was filled with a dense logic structure for a complex application. Interested, I took the stack of related drawings and sat down to see if I could figure out what the application was for.

As I followed the logic flow on the drawings, the hair on my neck raised. There before me, placed in my hands by God Almighty was the solution to the problem for the project I was working on!

Sure, it did require significant work to be implemented within the software and hardware environment of our control system but the principles could be applied exactly.

Sitting at my desk it was hard to control my emotions. I had just witnessed a miracle that was so specific and direct that I could not deny that I experienced a very real encounter with the God who provides - "…everything else will be given to you…."

Even as I finish this paragraph I am overwhelmed with a sense of God's goodness. It was mind-boggling that the Creator of the universe reached out to support me in my job so specifically. It was work that did not have any real world changing consequences, but He helped me because He is true to His Word! God's love, grace and mercy is hard to describe. It changes you forever. Even with the logic drawings in my hands it was hard to comprehend the relationship that God offers to all whom are willing to accept it.

> Greater love has no one than this, that someone lay down his life for his friends. You are my friends if you do what I command you. No longer do I call you servants, for the servant does not know what his master is doing; but I have called you friends, for all that I have heard from my Father I have made known to you.
> —John 15:13-15

God's provision when we seek Him is not an abstract, touchy-feely concept. It is a simple truth of cause and effect, if you dare step out of the boat onto the water and take God at His Word. The project ended in success. The Lord's purposes were beyond my thoughts and dreams though. This was just the start leading to a sequence of events that propelled my career forward.

~~~~~~

As my wife and I grew in our relationship with the Lord, we took on more responsibility at the church and became the leaders of the youth group. We did not have any children ourselves which had its advantages and disadvantages. On the one hand we were completely ill-prepared to deal with the youth in town at a church that had open doors for all.

In our youth, my wife and I were never confronted with the troubles and struggles experienced by some of the young people that frequented the group; definitively not with the same intensity and frequency. Drugs, sex, alcohol, abusive and absent parents, friend's suicides, teen pregnancy, lack of purpose, and little hope for the future as well as depression populated the list.

From our perspective there was little discipline and respect amongst the children in the youth group. Most of the kids that attended did not know God. We did not know what we let ourselves into; if we did, we probably would have steered clear and stayed firmly within our comfort zones.

Being 'non-parents' and foreigners gave us some 'street credibility' and thus allowed us to apply an approach which locals may not have been able to get away with. This was trial by fire but God showed His faithfulness to provide all that we needed to do His work in obedience. He taught us to depend on Him. God is always faithful to His Word.

The cares of this life often distract us and we put off acting on what God has instructed us to do. Instead of changing our circumstances for the better we don't allow God to do His part. He never leaves us or forsakes us but is with us in every situation. All we need to do is to be concerned about what God is concerned about.

We learned to, "Trust in the Lord with all your heart and do not lean on your own understanding" (Proverbs 3:5). Like all things we do for the sake of His Kingdom, our experience meant as much or more to ourselves as it did to those that were the beneficiaries of our ministry.

My wife is the people person in the family and with more time available she fulfilled the role of the main leader of the youth group. I did my part and all the technical setup, sound and video. The 'last stop' for any disciplinary issues was my department as well.

A wonderful team of youth leaders consisting of a girl and three boys formed part of the leadership team. Our first encounter with the young lady was when she arrived drunk at the youth group on a Friday night. We had to ask her to leave. She became our spiritual daughter, and as I am writing this, she is visiting from Scotland at our Houston home.

We initiated a policy of no tolerance. Some behaviors were just not allowed. For example, persons under the influence of any substance were asked to leave. A "three strikes and you're out" rule also applied. The approach of respect for authority, proceedings and the environment was non-negotiable. Anyone not abiding would have face the consequences.

Some would argue that our approach bordered on 'tough love'. It might have been tough, but it was love. A love that really cared about their futures and aimed to keep them from making less promising life choices or acquiring habits at a young age which would be hard to shake off later in life.

The youth used any leniency as a stepping stone towards asserting the kind of Friday night entertainment that they wanted, instead of what was good for them. In the beginning we did lose quite a number of attendees who thought the new regime was not to their liking. Although it was somewhat of a concern, it did not deter us from the path we had taken. We worked with the young people who attended and focused on equipping young leaders with the necessary spiritual and life skills. The young leaders were in a better position than we were, as adult leaders, to reach out to their peers and be age group role models. Given the responsibility, they flourished.

Purpose, meaning and belief form a powerful dynamic which caused us to venture beyond our diminished views of ourselves. Together with the Holy Spirit "...all things are possible for those whom believe" (Mark 9:23).

Soon others were attracted to what they experienced and they became an 'extended' part of the leadership team which we called the "Core Group."

A typical Friday night started with a pre-youth group meeting at 6:30 p.m. with a message for the leaders, to pray together and get ready for the night. The message, prayer and worship during this time were much more mature than was offered to the group during the evening. It wasn't long before the core youth group joined in this session. They turned up at church at 5 p.m. which later became closer to 3 p.m. after school was out. We thought it would be too intense for them, but they stayed and came back every week.

Why did they turn up early to a 'more godly' environment?

Because nothing attracts people like the true presence of God and His way of life. The biggest mistake one can make is to try and be people pleasing. Although it may lure people in for a time, it does not result in any lasting impact.

From my perspective any youth club, or church for that matter that does not put God and His Kingdom first and act out His teachings, is just another social club. There are many social clubs but only one true God.

The rules and boundaries based on the Bible together with tough love that did not compromise, were what the youth longed for. Mix in the practical application of the dynamic power of prayer manifesting before the eager young eyes, and you have a combination in which the Lord Jesus Christ does His work in a masterful way.

Many of the younger kids, even the ones who disappeared for weeks at times, are now part of the leadership team at the same youth group. Praise to God that the young leaders chose to remain in godly leadership positions and continue to serve in some ministry capacity.

As an engineer who is used to design, logic and preparation, I learned to lean more on the leading of the Holy Spirit than to depend on my own talents and skills. My skillset does not include all the tools required to deal with assignments from God.

I do still very much enjoy research, gaining knowledge, preparation and planning. None of these activities though will produce the revelation to bring a message, make a phone call or write an e-mail that brings a personal Word from God to the recipient at exactly the right time. Only obedience and sensitivity to God communicating makes this possible.

The involvement in the youth group changed me in many ways

including largely diminishing my fear of public speaking which later helped me in my career. Most importantly I learned that God will take care of your needs when you make yourself available to operate on behalf of His Kingdom.

It is of key importance to be able to communicate with God. I longed to communicate with Him in a more clear and specific manner. It appealed to my internal wiring as an engineer. I didn't mind the more abstract communication, but I much rather prefer clear instructions to which I can commit and proceed with certainty, following the Lord in the most effective way. Determined to develop this aspect I continued the journey.

Then he said to his disciples, "The harvest is plentiful, but the laborers are few; therefore pray earnestly to the Lord of the harvest to send out laborers into his harvest."

—Matthew 9:37-38

7

IT WORKS

Not communicating efficiently is only part of the hindrance to operate effectively as a believer. The more challenging part is to be obedient when God does speak clearly.

> What good is it, my brothers, if someone says he has faith but does not have works? Can *that* faith save him?
>
> — James 2:14 (emphasis added)

There is a significant difference between knowing the path and walking the path. It is a joy to support others in prayer and engage on the behalf of others who are walking the path. It is inspiring to see missionaries step out in faith to do God's work and few would argue that the act itself is not commendable. We love to hear and tell stories of people who stepped out for the Lord and are doing great things, just like we love to remember the heroes of the Bible.

What happens though when those missionaries that stepped out for the Lord 'fail' in human terms? Return to base (so to speak) with cap in hand, giving up on their vision. The typical first response would be to patronize those involved or question their faith and motives. Did they really hear from God or are they just freeloaders or lazy members of society without drive? Judgment is handed down, even if unknowingly.

The thought of being 'exposed' in this manner is enough to discourage most from augmenting their faith with action. This conclusion is based primarily on incorrect assumptions. These assumptions conclude that works of faith imply becoming a missionary in a foreign land, is bound to a specific assignment, or is an external activity from a person's daily environment. It is further assumed that a temporary setback or adjustment in an assignment negates the significance of the spiritual progress accomplished by the participants. This assumption fails to take into account the faithfulness and splendor of God's guardianship through the Holy Spirit. No effort sincerely exerted on God's behalf fails to develop the relationship with the Father, and in turn push back evil.

Stepping out in faith means just that: No safety net, and a fair amount of spiritual and natural opposition. Failure in human terms will leave you feeling naked, figuratively speaking. Without trying however one will never succeed. Opportunities are abundant all around us.

Living a Kingdom life requires an ever increasing level of faith in God's power and provision. It is scary but exhilarating as Peter realized when he stepped out of the boat. Stepping out of the boat is the only way to walk on water and experience God in the way the disciples did. Jesus walked on the water first and was there to help Peter when he struggled. Peter's struggle did not affect His relationship with Jesus in a negative manner. It showed Jesus the intent of Peter's heart and for Peter it confirmed that he will never be left on his own by his Lord to sink to the bottom.

I believe the time has come for God's people, in all areas of life, to wake up from the slumber and set our sights beyond the bottleneck restriction of the pulpit. The convenient dependency by believers on an individual for their spiritual development drip feeds the expansion of the Kingdom. It is time for Christians to take ownership of their individual spiritual development and relationship with God. Our effectiveness to positively impact the community should be based on a common resolve, ready to be deployed not only sequentially through the doors of the organized church, but from our homes in parallel.

Pastors, ministers and other spiritual leaders should not be sparse beacons of light, but nodes in a sea of illumination. Satan and the worldly media would struggle to identify a target to discredit in an expansive front.

> …But as for me and my house, we will serve the Lord.
> — Joshua 24:15 (extract)

~~~~~~~~~

For some, turning faith into works is easier than for others. Many people shy away from the unknown and are much more comfortable with a predictable routine in their lives.

During my career I specialized in safety systems for protecting lives, the environment and equipment. I followed the normal path of going to college, secure a job and work for a salary. Until recently I pretty much knew what to expect every month. I like to know what tomorrow brings and try to always plan ahead. My natural instinct is to avoid risk.

The confidence that enable us to move beyond our comfort zones into an area of risk is rooted in the faith given by God to every human being.

It is a chicken and egg situation. As I mentioned, one has to step out of the boat to know if it is possible to walk on water. The Lord often makes His will clear but less often explains the why and how. If we trust Him, we don't need to know why and how. Trusting Him is sufficient to enable us to fulfill His will, thus providing the proof that He can always be trusted.

After a few years of being involved with the church in Scotland we were presented with a major decision. My wife had a good job at a stationary and office supplies store in one of the neighboring towns. She soon distinguished herself and became the manager for the business department. Just as my wife had made the job her own, God came knocking. Being a great administrator and organizer she saw a real need at our church. The Lord started working in her heart. Together with all the new things we discovered in our walk with God it led her to a place where she felt that it was the Lord calling her to this ministry.

From a worldly point of view this pending life change would not make sense at all. After arriving with very little, we had worked ourselves into a position of financial stability. A place where we could live comfortably, start building up the contents of our home and maybe travel for vacation. As a young couple we were just at the beginning of our life journey.

Inevitably the conversation was initiated to consider God's call. Because of the spiritual journey that we were on, I neither accepted nor rejected the matter offhand. It allowed me to have more of an open mind. Yet as the head of the household and also carnal man this would be a case of guilty until proven innocent. In other words, let's look at the facts and see where it leads us to. The conclusions that we reached brought a strong case against any change of career for my wife.

The job at the church would be without any pay, besides covering expenses. We could have stopped the process just there and then but deep down we knew that the apparently valid evaluation process, even though it was helpful to arrange and provide metrics for our thoughts, was ultimately flawed when it came to spiritual matters. Why? Because it failed to take into account all the facts - facts that were locked in the future.

In normal day to day life we have to make many decisions. Many times important decisions have to be made based on incomplete or insufficient information. A good example of this is when at a very young age people have to decide what career path they want to pursue. This decision is made at an early stage when we really have inadequate information, experience and insight. Even after years of study I still did not know exactly what it would be like to be an engineer. How would I know at eighteen years of age that this would be the right decision? I didn't, but I made the best decision based on the information that I had at the time.

We have to make decisions. Worse than making a possible wrong decision is making no decision at all. If one makes a wrong decision it can still be changed, ultimately leading to an acceptable outcome. Making no decision at all, means one will never reach the correct destination and definitely not in a reasonable amount of time.

The Kingdom of God adds another dimension. God knows the end from the beginning. In His possession is the missing information required to enable a good decision with a very high probability of success. Why not with absolute certainty? We are human and imperfect and do not always hear correctly from God, maintain the required level of faith or act according to God's will as instructed. Does it matter? No. God can use any situation to bring something positive in our lives, if we choose to follow Him even in the mess we create for ourselves. What matters is that we try.

Ultimately the guidance of the Holy Spirit overrides everything else. Sometimes God works in the most powerful ways when it does not seem to make good sense.

In our situation we decided to seek the Lord for specific confirmation. The Lord complied. On her way back from work shortly after we asked the Lord to provide instruction, my wife listened to a sermon tape (yes, do you still remember those things?) that had been lying around for weeks. The message focused on these scripture verses,

> Do not lay up for yourselves treasures on earth, where moth and rust destroy and where thieves break in and steal, but lay up for yourselves treasures in heaven, where neither moth nor rust destroys and where thieves do not break in and steal. For where your treasure is, there your heart will be also
>
> — Matthew 6:19 -21

> Looking at the birds or the air: they neither show nor reap nor gather into barns, yet your heavenly Father feeds them. Are you not more value than they? And why are you anxious about clothing? Consider the lilies on the field, how they grow: they neither toil or spin
>
> — Matthew 6: 26, 28

Does this mean God does not want us to prosper? No. He wants all good things for us, but He has eternity in mind which is way beyond our imagination. Our life on earth is but a speck when compared to eternity.

As my wife listened to this message she knew that it was the Lord's answer to our prayers. After her explanation, I did not need further convincing; she knew in her heart. In the years to come we had bigger decisions to make and adopted the "three confirmations" rule which has worked well for us. This time it was pretty clear without three confirmations, and we decided to be obedient.

Delayed obedience is disobedience, a pastor friend told us. My wife resigned. It was difficult to explain to the people she worked with and with whom she had become friends. Many of them were religious but did not know God. The fact that my wife would not receive a salary was hard to grasp, with the obvious comment, "the church is taking advantage of your goodness." In a society where you are born into a religion without any real expectation this did not make sense.

The Lord is faithful, although His provision may not manifest within your expected timeframe. It became clear as time went on that the move was God's will. My wife was a blessing to the church and the people in the congregation. Our experience through the church was a blessing to us.

As time progressed the church received money from the local government and the state for the work that they were doing in the community and my wife eventually received a salary. It wasn't much but allowed us to engage in activities besides just living to work. This was our first taste of stepping out in faith in regard to the life we were building and more importantly listening for God's voice in major decisions.

We could have easily written off the 'answer' we received via the sermon on tape as coincidence. Before you can have an effective level of communication with the Lord, you have to believe that He wants to guide you when you inquire from Him and that He does this on a personal level.

> I have said these things to you in figures of speech. The hour is coming when I will no longer speak to you in figures of speech but will tell you plainly about the Father
>
> — John 16:25

God never tries to trick us, but Satan certainly likes playing mind games. The battlefield of the mind is the Christians' greatest obstacle. Satan will do his utter best to convince us that we did not hear from God, especially just after we make the decision to step out of the boat.

Faith must be transformed into belief that, "what He says will come to pass" (Mark 11:23 extract). This is accomplished through action or works of obedience that foster dependence and trust.

"... look, I shall put a fleece of wool on the threshing floor; if there is dew on the fleece only, and it is dry on all the ground, then I shall know that You will save Israel by my hand, as You have said."

—Judges 6:37

8

PROTOCOL DEFINITION

The reality that "The Great I AM" chooses to engage with us as normal believers is mind-boggling. I had established for myself that God communicates with His children. He does answer prayers and He provides specific guidance. I wondered if God only communicated in 'random' ways or if it could be more defined. Are broadcast type messages the only way He uses to communicate?

Were we destined to be listening stations that have to be alert to every visual and audible stimulus that permeates our personal space? Should we always be ready to intercept a packet of data that is destined for us with the help of the Holy Spirit? I was reminded of how God provided the solution to the engineering problem so tangibly with a physical drawing set. I never asked Him for this, but yet He provided an even more direct answer than what I could imagine.

I expected a fellow engineer to provide me with the solution through discussion. He did use human beings to deliver the drawing set to my desk, but His provision was more definitive than that. Could I influence the way that God communicates to me? I know it sounds presumptuous, but trained as an engineer I prefer the most efficient answer possible so I can 'get on with the job'. If the Lord had a purpose in delaying the answer it is fine with me; His ways are greater than my ways. However, if He chooses to answer immediately, could I minimize the time that I spent plodding in the dark?

The simple solution according to my logic was to establish an agreed communications protocol. Not for the Lord's benefit but for mine; the guy who needs Jesus to perfect his faith. The protocol would need to be bidirectional or include a data packet that is recognized as a message from the Lord. It should preferably include a unique packet of data, like a source internet address of a computer or a smart device. Confirmation that, "This is God."

With telecommunication devices, the speed of data transfer is negotiated and determined by the device with the lowest specification or slowest speed capability. It would make sense that we could request specific signs from God like Gideon did in the Bible, but enhanced for a technological environment, so we can 'get it'. To my personality this possibility was very appealing. My wife is very sensitive to the Holy Spirit in terms of 'getting a feeling'. I am better with concrete signs. Like Gideon, I am a fleece man.

The pursuit initiated my realization that God is the Lord of all things - spirit, man and nature. I later discovered that God also is also Lord of machines or systems. In fact every single particle in this universe is under His control. He is able to do all things, including engaging with His children in a way that they understand.

I was inspired to find my own 'calling card' or token. As an engineer and a numbers guy, I asked the Lord if His number, the number *seven*, could be my calling card or unique piece of data. *He obliged.*

~~~~~~

My first experience with the agreed protocol was ahead of one of our trips to South Africa to visit family. We were involved in a weekend field trip with the youth group in the countryside. Scheduled to depart to South Africa the following Thursday, we had it all planned out and hoped to cruise to our departure date.

My work however had other plans. I was asked to take a trip on short notice to an offshore gas production platform that required a change to the process safety system. The North Sea between Scotland and Norway is very unpredictable to say the least. The time of year was also notorious for fog which grounded helicopters used to transport workers offshore and back. Fog offshore could last from hours to several days.

I was stuck in the fog before and felt very concerned. As a good soldier I agreed to make the trip, which was supposed to last one day only.

I left the youth camp early on the Sunday afternoon to travel up to Aberdeen. Somewhat nervous, I arrived at the hotel, checked-in and received the key to my room. As I dragged myself to the elevator, I glanced at the little card envelope that held the electronic key: Room number, "7." A pulse of excitement was followed by the thought that maybe this was just coincidence.

While I stood staring at the large gold colored seven on the door, a peace came over me. I knew this was the Lord.

I completed the work I had to do without too much trouble. When I inquired about the time the helicopter was scheduled to arrive however, I was met with some worrying news. The company had been experiencing problems in transferring people off some platforms for several days because of the fog. Now that they could finally fly to those areas, the company faced a backlog of people that needed transport back to shore. In short, they did not have a seat available. As a vendor who just arrived offshore I was seen as less of a priority.

If I did not get back to shore that day, I would miss our flight. My heart sank. I politely reminded my contact person that I only agreed to go offshore on condition that they would take me back to shore in time for my vacation.

To lose my nerve would not have helped. I walked away to get a cup of tea. In the tea shack, the Holy Spirit reminded me of the "7" on my hotel room door. Peace came over me. God said that everything will work out and He is faithful. About an hour later I was informed that they diverted another helicopter to make a stop at the platform especially for me, otherwise I would have had no chance. I needed to get my stuff immediately and get ready. "You are very lucky", said my contact. I could see in his eyes he meant it. Luck had nothing to do with it.

This sign or calling card has become part of my life. Since then, I have expanded the parameters of the agreed protocol but the number *seven* still features as the primary method for specific confirmation. Countless times I have sat at table seven or a variation, received order number seven or a variation, check number seven etc. In the tough times when the battle was fierce, I called into question if this was all in my head. My wife would calmly affirm, "You know, I have made a habit of checking and I hardly ever get the number seven in anything. Keep the faith; It is not just in your head."

We all need somebody to help strengthen our faith regardless of how strong we are, Satan is very skilled at hitting us exactly where it hurts to bring about as much doubt in our minds as he can.

Without faith we cannot please God. Doubt is the kryptonite of our relationship with the Father. The enemy will call into question the very foundation of the revelation we receive from the Father, our vision, our identity. "No servant is greater than his master", Jesus said. Before Jesus started His ministry on earth, the very core of Satan's attack was Jesus' identity. "*If* you are the Son of God.....", was his opening salvo for Jesus. For me, "*If* God spoke to you, why ....", continues to be Satan's onslaught.

There are so many occasions that the Lord honored my 'protocol' request. One of my favorite moments, when God utilized the requested 'protocol', was when we decided to have dinner with a pastor and his wife. The Lord led us to another church home and there were no hard feelings or ill words spoken when we left their church. My wife suggested that we needed to go to dinner a number of months after we left. I did not agree at first. From my perspective there were no ill feelings and we had all moved on to other things. I wasn't sure if arranging a dinner out of the blue would send the right message.

My wife convinced me, but even while waiting in the car I did not really look forward to the dinner. I was wondering about the necessity of what we were doing when my eye caught the odometer reading. "...*seventy seven*", I read out loud. I now had the assurance that my wife heard from God. We had a great dinner and fellowship together. The bill came and there it was…..In a restaurant with less than fifty tables we sat at table number *"seventy seven."*

I don't think the Lord changed the table number in the system that time (anything is possible), but He ensured that we sat down at that specific table.

God does not always respond as requested, sometimes He wants us to make our own decisions and get on with life. He does however often provide the signs that we ask for, much like He did for Gideon. I have met a number of people that have discovered their own calling card with the Lord over the years, be it a heart shape, flower, number or something else.

Jesus is the same yesterday, today and tomorrow but His methods are dynamic, personal and on par with the times we live in.

Do not be overcome by evil, but overcome evil with good.

—Romans 12:21

9

INTERSECTION

The Holy Spirit influences the hearts and minds of men and women that have received Jesus Christ as their Lord and Savior. Likewise an absence of the Holy Spirit leaves the door open for either the sinful nature embodied by the flesh, or evil to sway behavior with little resistance.

In response to our own transgressions, we love to blame Satan or circumstance. When we are on the receiving end of an evil deed, the same latitude is not afforded at all. The transgressor's character is typically ripped to shreds, while we demand that the perpetrator accept responsibility for their actions and make up for the indiscretion that was committed.

It is important that we are always alert to the continuous battle between good and evil. In any situation where evil presents itself, the souls of all parties involved are exposed to lethal infection.

Evil has many faces and can present itself as terror, seduction or what appear as beautiful and good. The intent of evil is always the same – ruthless destruction.

And no wonder, for even Satan disguises himself as an angel of light.

—2 Corinthians 11:1

The thief comes only to steal and kill and destroy.

— John 10:10

If not prepared, the ferocity of the assault can eliminate whatever belief or revelation one had. The purpose is to keep us captive in a form of religion that lacks the power of the Kingdom.

~~~~~~

Evil will wait until the most opportune moment to launch an all-out assault. My wife and I received heart-wrenching news from a medical specialist in the midst of our season dedicated to youth ministry. The doctor informed us that we would have difficulty conceiving children. Our chances for natural procreation were very slim according to the test results.

I had to spend a significant amount of time working away from home soon after we received the news. The team stayed in a small privately owned hotel that had only a few rooms. It was a great place to stay with a very homely atmosphere. My days were spent testing equipment scheduled to be shipped offshore. The customers were great people to work with and we all saw eye-to-eye, which allowed the days to go by fairly quickly between weekends.

I enjoyed the team's company after hours even if it was difficult at times. I did not consume much alcohol and frequently excused myself early while the rest were carrying on late into the evening. This was a source of friction on many occasions as nobody wanted a capable witness of what was said and done under the influence. The social occasions were probably the most difficult part of working with the team. I wanted to engage but not comply. It was hard being from another culture, but even harder not being seen as 'one of the guys' to this extent, since we worked so well together.

Inevitably the conversations would lead to why I was not drinking like the others, insinuating that I was not being social. One particular night the banter between the lines started to surface. We talked about a lot of things and I had an opportunity to testify about God. They knew that we did not have any children yet and one of the customers alluded to the fact that I was not a real man. I decided it was best for me to remove myself from the situation and retire for the night. This did not go down well.

I was still heartbroken for myself, but more so for my wife, who has the characteristics of a great mother. It was difficult to work away from home. It meant that we had to deal with this still raw issue separated by a few hundred miles during the week.

The loud banging of fists on my door woke me up shortly after I fell asleep. It was followed by a tirade of abuse. Between the cursing, I could make out that the person was questioning my manhood, suggesting that I was homosexual and therefore did not want to be intimate with my wife. He went on to shout out, "You religious freak. If there is a God that cares why don't you have children?" He implied that following Jesus was a waste of time. Many of the things said could be heard by everybody in the small building and hit exactly where it hurt.

The Father blessed me with His grace and the Holy Spirit enabled me to see clearly. This was not the customer blowing off steam; it was a demonic attack intent on destroying my relationship with the Father and to push me over the edge to curse God and cast off my faith as dead religion. With my eyes on Jesus, I managed to forgive.

The next morning at breakfast I had no ill feeling at all against the perpetrator - a mere man held captive by deception. Confronting him would have given Satan another chance of victory by destroying a good relationship through bitterness and resentment. Satan himself would disappear into the shadows proud of the two lives he so easily derailed.

In that hotel room I was faced with evil banging on the door, but I was armed with the truth. If I had vented my anger and blamed God, I am pretty sure evil would have found a way into my inner sanctuary and wreaked havoc.

My wife and I separated ourselves immediately for a weekend after we initially received the bad news from the specialist. We fasted, prayed and drew close to God. The Father responded with the truth. He loved us and the burden that we faced was not because of anything we had done. We needed to depend on Him and not take matters in our own hands.

The Holy Spirit guided my wife to a very specific verse revealing that she would pray for particular women to bear children. Even while the wounds were still raw, the Lord brought the women He had in mind across her path; she prayed for them and they became pregnant.

Instead of resentment she felt deep joy for the women when they conceived, sometimes after supporting them for months. This was made possible only by the power of the Holy Spirit.

Society teaches us to be envious or at least apathetic towards the joy of others, especially if we pursue the same goals. "Why do they deserve it and why not me?" dominates the thinking of carnal man.

We received the heart-wrenching news on Good Friday, which the cynic would find ironic. God however initiated a journey that gave us a glimpse of the sacrificial love that Jesus displayed for us on the cross. Love, covered in the blood of an innocent man and absent of any resentment that He had to pay the price for others to be set free.

> Although he was a son, he learned obedience through what he suffered. And being made perfect, he became the source of eternal salvation to all who obey him
>
> —Hebrews 5:8

~~~~~

Many never recover from the relentless onslaughts from Satan; often because they are ill prepared and their mindset are not right. One must be armed with the truth, prepared that a battle may ensue at any time and accept that you may lose some battles.

Significant fights can be a lengthy war. The key is to realize that losing a battle does not mean that the war is lost. The war is won by perseverance. To serve Christ is to take up your cross on a daily basis. God will use even the defeats to teach and develop us.

My prayer is that the stories contained in this book will encourage you to move beyond where you thought you could go in your relationship with the Lord and to win the wars. Faith should not be driven by events, but by God's character - dependable and trustworthy.

For a day in your courts is better than a thousand elsewhere. I would rather be a doorkeeper in the house of my God than dwell in the tents of wickedness.

—Psalm 84:10

The foundation of a believers' joy, is the knowledge of a loving Father with whom we will be forever. It may take some time to turn this knowledge into belief, especially when you have been deeply hurt. The presence of the Lord brings a depth of inner healing that is impossible to achieve without the power of the Holy Spirit.

Communicating with the Father in the throne room, enable us to transcend temporary earthly despair.

The steps of a man are established by the Lord, when he delights in his way;

— Psalm 37:23

10

CROSSING OVER

After ten years in Scotland we felt in our spirit that a life change was imminent, but we were not sure what the change would entail. I worked on a mega project that involved personnel from all over the world. The budget was enormous for a control system project. It involved the complete scope of control, fire and gas, safety and monitoring systems. The process utilized advanced technology and the objective was to build a massive scalable system that was fully integrated and operable from a single user interface. It was a huge undertaking and took years to complete.

Even though I had worked on many projects, I never worked on a project of this magnitude. I was the designated Lead Engineer for one part of the project.

The key personnel were from the United Kingdom and Europe. Although modern technology was used to communicate all the time, a significant amount of travel and work away from home was still required. It remains more efficient to locate multiple interested parties who need to brainstorm and agree on design and requirements at the same location. I had to travel to Europe and London multiple times and could only return for the weekends.

After working on the project for a period of time, I became aware of opportunities in Australia and North America. Both the Perth and Houston offices advised that they could accommodate me. This would be a big change for me and especially my wife who had made many good friends (some are like family) in Scotland and built a new life in the preceding decade.

During this same time period my wife and I moved to a more prominent role in the church leadership and were faced with some very challenging situations. Many of the persons involved were much older than us. This added to the challenge as we came from a culture where older equaled wiser by default.

The Lord used this time to mold us into much more mature leaders and improved our people skills. I went through a crash course to prepare me for what lay ahead in my career. Just like the messages that I presented at church increased my confidence in speaking in front of people, I was now taught to lead sternly and to be assertive regardless of the age of those that I engaged with, no matter how difficult the circumstances. I acted with respect but also with confidence, pursuing the best way forward. It was necessary to be constantly aware of what Jesus would have done instead of what my flesh suggested.

God stretched me to develop skills that most people never really get a chance to learn until they get promoted to a level where it is required. The Lord will prepare and train us regardless of our fears and comforts, if we are obedient to His voice. He is the God of growth and development. If you have stopped developing at any point in your life, you probably let your relationship with God grow stagnant.

In the midst of some very emotional situations we had a hard choice to make. It felt like we were sandwiched between difficulties from every angle. As an engineer the logical way to make a decision is the scientific approach and we created a spreadsheet that contained the pros and cons of relocating to North America and Australia respectively. It was hard to make up our minds and we used this method in an attempt to arrive at a clear and unemotional conclusion. We did not succeed.

The score in both columns totaled to a 50/50 result. "Now this is just great", I remarked to my wife sarcastically. We would need to make up our minds with no help from the spreadsheet. There I was, equipped with prior experience of God's involvement in my career and in ministry, but still not petitioning the Lord first for an answer.

Somehow I thought I was responsible for coming to a conclusion. Surely I could not leave the basics to God. Sometimes, it is as if a foggy mist takes over my mind and I forget what God had done on my behalf before. No wonder the Bible tells us that we should tell our children and generations following us of the great deeds that the Lord has done. It is uncanny how easily we forget the cornerstones of our personal relationship with God and face the future as if no past existed, instead of being energized by the feats that God accomplished on our behalf.

I asked God to forgive me for not seeking His council and petitioned Him to clearly speak to me about moving to Texas or Australia. Importantly, I was expecting Him to speak and remained alert.

The next morning I arrived at work and read a daily devotional online before starting the day. The way the Lord responded was awesome. The devotional relayed the story of a pastor who flew a small aircraft from South America to the United States over the Gulf of Mexico. There was no radio communication and the pilot was surrounded by complete darkness. Every direction looked the same in the night time. When he saw the lights of Houston Texas, he was filled with joy. It did not matter what the spiritual application of the devotion was, that portion was for me. The Lord decided that this time He would just tell me straight. All I had to do is believe that He had spoken.

I know many people take issue with daily devotions and argue that Christians will milk the answer to a need or question out of the devotion and determine their lives by it. Almost like a crystal ball. I understand this point of view and agree. Like with many things in life that disappoint us, we too often disregard the good with the bad. Because something caused us harm does not mean that it is inherently bad. It may just be that we did not use it the right way, did not have the right skills or did not have the right relationship with the Lord.

Because I felt that the Lord spoke so clearly I did not urgently seek a second confirmation but kept my eyes open. The enemy immediately tried to counteract the word of the Lord. I received a phone call from Australia only a day or two later presenting a good proposition. I declined as the Lord was steering to Houston and not Perth, but almost immediately started to doubt if I made the right choice. The phone rang again only minutes later. I wondered if this was my chance to reconsider. It was quite the opposite. On the line was an old acquaintance from college. We did not have any contact with him for a long time, but somehow he found out that we were considering moving to Houston. He phoned, at God's appointed time, to inform us of a friend of his that worked and stayed in Houston. His friend's house was on the market and we could perhaps consider buying it.

The timing was immaculate and I knew this was the second confirmation from the Lord. However hearing from God is just one part of the journey. The enemy just started his campaign and we had to stand firm in our prayers, "Your will be done on earth as in heaven"

It was the beginning of 2008 and the mortgage crisis that hit the United States of America was spilling over to the United Kingdom and Europe. The housing market boom was quickly starting to fade and we knew we had to move quickly. We immediately put our house on the market. After discussions with the Houston office it was estimated that I could start with them at roughly the end of the first quarter.

Everything looked great and seemed to be lining up. In a short while a couple from one of the adjacent towns came to look at our house and wanted to buy it immediately. The realtor was very positive and we were excited praising the Lord for His goodness and immediate assistance. Only a day or two later the realtor informed us that the couple were having some family problems and would not proceed with the transaction.

The process of getting us relocated to the USA, including obtaining visas and other documentation seemed to take forever. What should have taken three months took eight months. It was a really difficult time. Everyone knew that I should have left a long time ago. Most thought it was not going to happen and that I was fooling myself. At one time I thought the Lord kept us there to help lead the church through a tough time. I think He did use us in that capacity but He was not the cause of the interference.

About three months after the process started my wife had given up her job at the church in anticipation of the relocation and was ready to leave. Because of all the delays she found a temporary job at a demolition company. There she met a woman who had married and lived in South Africa and God used even this time for good.

Nothing that we experienced indicated that our plans would work out. Even if all the job related issues would have been resolved, it would be very difficult to depart if our home was not sold. The housing market was getting worse and worse as the days went by.

The owner of the demolition company invited us to join him, together with our new friends from South Africa, to attend a concert performance in the Glasgow Theater. Dinner was on the agenda just before the performance. Normally we would have looked forward to the social engagement but at the time we were dreading more questions about why we were still resident in Scotland. It added pressure to justify what probably seemed to non-believers like a lack of action by our 'loving' God. After dinner, that went smoothly, we excitedly proceeded to take our places for the performance. The artist together with the orchestra appeared on stage. After greeting the audience he opened with the words, "…we just came back from a performance in Houston Texas, where we had such a great time….!" My wife and I looked at each other in disbelief. With the third confirmation of our destination, I knew God was still on the move even though it felt like He had gone on vacation.

The Lord most often does not remove us from the fire in the time frame we would prefer but He is always right next to us. His purposes will be fulfilled if we only believe.

Do not fear, only believe

— Mark 5:36

Those unassuming words from an artist were the surge that was needed to jump-start our pulses once again. In expectation that God would communicate and guide us through, we continued to cling to our faith even though interest in our home seemed non-existent.

AT THE EDGE OF THE WATER

I hoped that when the Lord confirmed our move so clearly for the third time that everything would run smoothly from then onwards. Maybe God's words and the breakthrough we prayed for had finally manifested in the natural and the situation would be completely resolved in the morning. The next morning came and nothing changed. Nothing that we could detect with our natural senses indicated any improvement in the situation.

God intended to strengthen our faith, confirm His provision and ensure our complete dependence on Him. His confirmation did have the desired effect on our hearts and minds. It reset our stress levels and helped us not to pursue "Ishmael" instead of waiting on "Isaac" as the Lord instructed.

God desires that we trust Him completely. Only then can He truly trust us to pursue His will on earth and not weaken it by our own intentions. When we are weak God proves Himself.

But he said to me, "My grace is sufficient for you, for my power is made perfect in weakness." Therefore I will boast all the more gladly of my weaknesses, so that the power of Christ may rest upon me. For the sake of Christ, then, I am content with weaknesses, insults, hardships, persecutions, and calamities. For when I am weak, then I am strong.

— 2 Corinthians 12:9-10

After *seven* months, the process to relocate had progressed enough that management decided to get me started on my next project which would be executed from Houston.   I worked remotely (from Scotland) on the front end engineering documentation for the project. After a few weeks the project entered the last stages of the initial work that was done between the end-user and the engineering contractor; it was time for the core members of our project team to engage. I joined the team for a one week trip to California to meet up with the customer. After the initial trip I returned to Scotland and continued to work on the project remotely.

The lawyers informed us that our visa applications were complete and submitted to the US embassy in London. I booked an appointment at the embassy for the interview that was required prior to approval. Finally there was some traction and the end was in sight with regards to the formalities to enable us to live and work in the US, for the duration of the project.

The sense of relief was short lived, as our focus changed to the other big hurdle that was firmly in place, our house was still not sold and interest dwindled. We changed realtors and did everything we possibly could to sell the house. The pressure was mounting.

My wife and I travelled to London for the interview, wondering when the Lord would come through. There wasn't much time left. The relocation activities accelerated while the housing market continued to slow down.

The embassy interview went smoothly and the visa was approved. From the employer's point of view, there was nothing holding us back.

We stopped at a fast food restaurant before heading back to the hotel a few blocks away. Conversation was muted. Our thoughts were occupied by worry, "What now God?"

The house-hunting trip in Houston was scheduled to go ahead a week after our visit to the embassy. The only logical choice would be to ask for a delay until our house was sold. We had no idea how long it would take and it might have required us to live separately for some time. It did not make any sense to go house-hunting if we could not move.

With nothing meaningful to say, I went to the restroom, far removed from an environment that one would expect to be conducive to invite the presence of the Lord. I cried out to God once again and prayed, "Lord, everything feels out of control. Should I proceed and go on the house-hunting trip with my wife or should we postpone until we find a buyer?"

I clearly heard a voice in my head, one of the few times in my life, "Just do it!"

Back in the restaurant area, I shared with my wife what I felt the Lord said. She accepted the Word with some skepticism. She is such a great supporter but also cares for me deeply and was fearful that my eagerness to follow the Lord was clouding my judgment. The Lord knew this, and He also knew that we would need each other to push through as a united front.

We followed the printed map that I held in my hands while we walked back to our hotel through some narrow London streets. With my eyes focused on the map and the sidewalk, I made a sharp right turn at the corner of the building at the end of the block. I ended up facing the doors of a store.

I was tricked by the entrance of the store. It was positioned at a forty five degree angle, slicing off the corner of the building. Somewhat bewildered I stopped and looked up. Right above us was a giant Nike® sign with the slogan, "JUST DO IT®." From our perspective God provided us with the second confirmation and this time my wife was a witness. I did not have to say anything. She knew.

A third confirmation was provided soon after we arrived home. I was working at home and switched on Christian television while taking a lunch break. A British evangelist was presenting a message and his humorous approach caught my attention. He said, "Sometimes we wonder if we should move forward with what the Lord had instructed and we look for all the stars to align instead of believing." He concluded "Sometimes you have to… just do it!"

God in His grace and mercy made it clear that despite what was in front of us we should proceed and go ahead as planned with no delays.

The numbers did not add up for this engineer but he closed his eyes and dipped his feet in the water. Like the Israelites under Joshua's leadership, the waters did not stop flowing before we started to cross the river.

And Joshua said, "Here is how you shall know that the living God is among you and that he will without fail drive out from before you the Canaanites, the Hittites, the Hivites, the Perizzites, the Girgashites, the Amorites, and the Jebusites. Behold, the ark of the covenant of the Lord of all the earth is passing over before you into the Jordan. Now therefore take twelve men from the tribes of Israel, from each tribe a man. And when the soles of the feet of the priests bearing the ark of the Lord, the Lord of all the earth, shall rest in the waters of the Jordan, the waters of the Jordan shall be cut off from flowing, and the waters coming down from above shall stand in one heap."

— Joshua 3:10-13

IMMERSION

Jetlagged we waited for the relocation consultant to pick us up at the hotel in Houston as arranged. We were tired and braced ourselves for adapting to a new culture and a very hectic week ahead. God was one step ahead of us and prepared the way.

A very pleasant and helpful consultant greeted us. We clicked so well that we eventually became friends. When she started her car, the radio came on playing Christian songs that were very familiar to us. The consultant quickly adjusted the volume and asked if it was acceptable to us if we listened to the local Christian radio station. With one voice we said, "YES!"

We felt right at home and knew we were in good hands; not all consultants were so up front about their faith. It appeared that faith was important to this one.

The realtor was wonderful too and we saw quite a few homes in a very short time. My wife and I each had our own clipboard that we used to make notes and scored each house individually. Our hosts thought this was very impressive and amusing as they had never seen anything like that before. Once again we made our list, which was good, but the effort would be upstaged by the Lord - again!

So Jesus said to them, "Truly, truly, I say to you, the Son can do nothing of his own accord, but only what he sees the

Father doing. For whatever the Father does, that the Son does likewise.

— John 5:19

It is more important and much more efficient to be sensitive to the Father and find out what He is doing and join in, rather than asking Him to bless our plans. We should only pursue our way as an alternative not as the rule. Jesus set the example by doing only what He saw the Father doing.

Our heads were spinning and the time left to make a decision was short. We could have rented a home, but we believed it would be a lack of faith and disobedient to God, which in turn could lead to complications. We did not know what the future entailed. God only provided instruction for the next phase.

We sat in the back seat of the realtor's car at the end of a long day and long week when her phone rang. She sounded surprised and a little suspicious in her conversation with the party on the other end. A new home with all the upgrades and kitchen implements included had become available at a good price.

We headed straight over to the home builder's office. The agent was a very pleasant man, very successful, but down to earth. In between being briefed about the house, the conversation touched on principles and topics that resonated with our beliefs.

We were somewhat disappointed initially when we arrived at the house. Only the frame without any walls was presented to us. We nicknamed the house, "the sticks" As we walked through what would be the front door however, we both felt in our spirit that this was our home. I did not think my wife would consider the house because there was very little to see, but she felt the same way I did from the start.

A visiting speaker at our church, with the gift of public prophecy, spoke a Word over me before we left Scotland. Part of the Word declared that in a season of my life I would be like an Oak tree, but different from the ones we were familiar with in Scotland. That Oak tree did not shed its leaves in winter. This was both uncommon to me and the person that brought the Word, but she confirmed that the Word was accurate. I took the message and tucked it away in my memory for future reference.

As we walked through the frame of the house there was a single tree in the back yard. The relocation consultant remarked, "…it is a kind of Oak tree but it does not shed all its leaves in the winter…" Those words, together with what we both felt in our spirit were adequate confirmation. We went ahead and paid a sizable deposit to secure the home, knowing that there was still no buyer in sight for our home in Scotland.

From Houston we travelled to California. I worked during the day and my wife spent the time at the hotel room researching mortgages, interfacing with the realtor in the UK and doing some sightseeing.

Once the excitement of the house-hunt dissipated, the pressure again started to build to get our house in Scotland sold. After several days a little panic started to set in and we reached out to our parents to see if they could help us out financially in the short-term since our funds were locked up in the house in Scotland. They were very kind and agreed to help which relieved some of the pressure. A small voice inside of me however said that we were not being obedient to God and the lack of faith would keep us from receiving all the Lord's blessings that He had in store for us.

We celebrated our tenth wedding anniversary while we were in California and decided to drive inland to the Napa valley where we took a balloon ride. After a great day we stopped over for the night in Palm Springs. Most of our discussions that evening focused on making plans to ensure everything worked out. Just in case that the Lord meant we needed to make it happen when He instructed, "Just do it"

Sunday morning arrived and we switched on the television set in the motel room. It was tuned in on a local Christian station, like the alarm clock radio in the long stay hotel where we stayed upon our initial arrival from Houston. This was somewhat odd. God spoke to us both times when we first switched on the devices. In that motel room the Father gave us a real scolding about not trusting Him, through a very passionate pastor speaking with authority.

We realized that God was very serious about His instructions, and although He loved us, He seemed pretty unhappy.

The cracks in my armor typically appeared under pressure when I had lost confidence in my ability to sustain the required level of faith. When things did not go my way I felt my faith was not strong enough for what was required. I never doubted God's power, but because I did not see the results yet, the only possible conclusion was it had to be my lack of faith.

That was erroneous thinking. Jesus is, "...the founder and perfecter of our faith..." (Hebrews 12:2). All we need to do is to be obedient even if the manifestation of God's Word is not fully visible yet.

To deflect responsibility I could have made a statement at that juncture alluding to the fact that I was only a human being, who had failed. If I was completely honest with myself though, I would have admitted that I was a servant of the Lord and that disobedience on my side had a negative impact on the Kingdom of God. We are to act out the will of God on earth as He commanded.

Often we pray the prayer, "Your will be done on earth as it is in heaven" but do not follow through.

Back in Scotland, the days went by very quickly until time was up. I traveled to Houston but my wife had to stay for another two weeks to allow the shipping company to pack the contents of our home into a container.

The Lord left His calling card for me upon my arrival at the office. My desk in the Houston office was on floor number *seven* while the rest of the group was located on the eighth floor.

After a week in Houston, with one week remaining before my wife would depart from Scotland, the house was still not sold and the flames in the furnace felt scorching hot. My wife's flight was booked for the next Sunday morning. We had *seven* days to the deadline and doubt was pounding on the door.

That Saturday morning, for the first time I can remember, I could not get out of bed. My body was exhausted by stress. I felt that I was at my wits end and there was nothing I could do. Curled in a ball on the bed I called out to the Lord. I felt He spoke to my heart telling me that even though the flames were extremely hot, I would not burn.

...so that the tested genuineness of your faith—more precious than gold that perishes though it is tested by fire—may be found to result in praise and glory and honor at the revelation of Jesus Christ.

— 1 Peter 1:7

He answered and said, "But I see four men unbound, walking in the midst of the fire, and they are not hurt; and the appearance of the fourth is like a son of the gods."

— Daniel 3:25

107

Not wanting to get out of bed, I browsed my personal e-mails. The Holy Spirit reminded me of an e-mail that my brother sent me several months before. At the time my brother thought it could be of help to us. He reminded me again a couple of months later but I put it on the backburner - again. Since that time I have learned that my brother has a gift for bringing instruction from the Lord and I have to treat his messages accordingly.

I listened to the message from the hyperlink. It was an audio message regarding prayer. About halfway through the first hour I realized that I had seen the teacher on television before. It was during a lunch break when I was working at home back in Scotland. The part of his message that I saw was very interesting but I switched the television off to go back to work. I did not realize at the time that God was trying to get this message to me.

One of the sessions relayed the story of a man that wanted to buy a specific house in his town for years. The man felt that the Lord said to him it was his house. The house however never went up for sale and the owner living in the house at the time would not sell it when approached. After a long period of prayer, the man wanting the house was ready to give up. The Holy Spirit spoke to him and said that instead of praying for the house, he should pray that the Lord would bless the incumbent owner and resolve any problems the owner had.

God had already answered the man's prayer a long time ago but required him to be obedient and not focus on himself but his 'neighbor'. Not long after he started praying for the needs of the home owner instead of his own, the house was sold.

There was no doubt that this teaching applied to our situation. I realized that like Jesus, the Father expected us to put others first. That was the key.

I spent the following week praising the Lord for having answered my prayers already instead of begging Him to answer them. I prayed for the couple that was going to buy our house when it initially went on the market.

For *seven* days, instead of listening to the radio in the car, I worshipped. Instead of watching television at night I prayed both in the natural and in the Spirit. *Seven* days passed and it was the Saturday before the Sunday that my wife would depart from Scotland. Our home belongings were packed and my wife was arranging some décor in the empty rooms. We hoped that staging the house in this way would help to sell it.

Late that Saturday night Scotland time, I received a phone call from my wife. She was very excited. The couple who wanted to buy our home so many months ago unexpectedly walked through the front door and agreed to buy the house. I could not believe what I heard. We did not have any contact with them in months!

Disbelief changed to awe and I fell to my knees and thanked God. He is Almighty. That experience changed my perspective and I realized that it is never too late for the Lord. Even though the situation could probably have been resolved some time ago, God never gave up guiding us to receive His blessing. God was communicating all the time, but in the rush and busyness of life I neglected to listen to what He was saying. I promised myself, "Never again!"

We had already appointed a local solicitor with legal rights to sign any paperwork on our behalf and my wife left Scotland on the Sunday morning.

The next challenge was to get closure on the transaction and have the funds transferred to our account. All of this needed to happen in time for us to close the transaction on our new home.

The solicitor in Scotland diplomatically told us that it was highly unlikely that it would all happen in time. The process normally took four weeks. After two weeks we received an e-mail from the solicitor stating that everything was settled and the transaction was completed! She added that she never personally experienced a home sale process that completed so quickly.

We were set to take possession of our new home on the *seventeenth* of December. The only problem now would be to get the furniture in time or at least a bed to sleep on. The estimated minimum time for the shipment was six weeks, not considering the possibility of stormy seas. Six weeks shipping time would be two weeks too late for us to move in to our new home.

The week before we hoped to move in, I phoned the shipping company to get an update on the schedule. I was informed that the shipment would arrive early and delivery at our house would be possible from the *seventeenth* of December onward - exactly on time!

Praise God Almighty. Going through the process made me acutely aware of how capable our Father is and how much He cares. One thing I am sure of is that if God has spoken and His saints are willing to follow His instructions, nothing can stand against us.

God's instructions could include patience, prayer, actions or perseverance together with spiritual warfare. The critical part is waiting on the Lord and keeping the communication channel open. If you are like me, you need Jesus to strengthen you and perfect your faith.

Come now, you who say, "Today or tomorrow we will go to such and such a city, and spend a year there and engage in business and make a profit." Yet you do not know what your life will be like tomorrow. You are just a vapor that appears for a little while and then vanishes away. Instead, you ought to say, "If the Lord wills, we will live and also do this or that."

—James 4:13-15

11

BREAKING GROUND

With the move from the United Kingdom to the United States behind us our focus was to establish ourselves in the new environment. Even though the challenges were less daunting than we had just experienced, God was still providing His input as we broke ground.

Our first priority after we settled into our home was to find a church to attend and meet likeminded people. Our Scotland experience taught us that the closest church to home may not necessarily be the church that the Lord wanted us to go to.

Although the state of Texas and also the Houston area have no shortage of churches, there weren't any located in our immediate vicinity. The region we moved to was on the western outskirts of the greater Houston area. We started the search online and were pleasantly surprised at first by the sheer number of churches that popped up. The pleasant feeling turned to dismay as we wondered how we could survey all the churches to find the one that was right for us. After first researching their doctrines online we attended a different church every Sunday. We sat at the back, able to do our reconnaissance while remaining mostly anonymous.

One of the first stops was the church that I attended the week prior to our house being sold in Scotland. At that time the church displayed a big sign, advertising that they would show a documentary about Intelligent Design. I was very interested in the subject matter, which covered the alleged discrimination against supporters of the Intelligent Design theory in the scientific community and specifically higher education institutions. My assumption was that if this church was interested in current affairs, I would probably feel at home there.

The Lord knew my train of thought and He set up the bait to be ready the day after I had started my week of prayer. After one of the most stressed-out days of my life, hungry for the Lord's presence and comfort, I arrived about an hour too early at church. I didn't mind and neither did the very friendly and welcoming staff. I found a seat somewhere in the middle and listened to the worship team going through their warm-up session.

The time went by quickly and the service started with a reading of a chapter from the book of Psalms. The Word is the foundation of our faith and reading it before anything else set the tone for the whole service. On this particular Sunday the reading was from Psalm 91, the same psalm that I shared during the last message I presented at the church in Scotland.

He who dwells in the shelter of the Most High will abide in the shadow of the Almighty. I will say to the Lord, "My refuge and my fortress, my God, in whom I trust."

— Psalm 91:1-2

God was communicating to me. He reminded me of the words that I relayed to our church in Scotland with so much belief. The Father suggested that He had our move to Houston under control. We were aware that the church was perhaps only purposed on that day to serve as a reminder to me, but I wanted to share the church with my wife.

As we walked from the parking lot to the front entrance of the church, a friendly voice greeted my wife. It was the salesman from the store where we bought a washer and drier earlier in the same week. He just happened to be a member of the same church we chose to attend that Sunday! Now we knew why our buying experience was such a pleasure.

Even though my wife and I both really enjoyed the Bible-based church service, we kept on searching. We visited a number of churches and enjoyed all but one where it was evident that the pastor was more concerned about upsetting the congregation than preaching the Word as it is written. I wondered how we were ever going to decide as each church displayed a specific spiritual strength.

A week or two later my wife mentioned something 'weird' that happened to her. She was looking for a locksmith via an internet search engine when a church popped up as one of the top results. Although my wife did not look into it any further at the time, this strange occurrence immediately drew my attention as a possible God initiated event.

It took some digging through the browser history to call up the old search result page. The name of the church was listed amongst a host of locksmiths as my wife described before.

The next Sunday we decided to attend this church. A big white church was prominent on the right-hand side when we turned off the main road. The sign however was not for the church we were looking for. We continued down the narrow road around the back and came upon some smaller buildings with fewer than ten vehicles outside.

A temporary banner indicated that it was in fact the church we were looking for. We glanced at each other and the same thought crossed our minds. The church was very small and there was no way that we would be able to hide in the back (so to speak), while assessing the church. We slowly drove through the parking lot debating what we should do and drove out the other side.

"We can always come back another Sunday", we said in unison. Both of us felt strongly that we were not being obedient, but still chose to attend another church that Sunday.

Two weeks later on a Saturday afternoon, one of our neighbors approached us when we arrived home, to find out if we were settling in successfully. At the end of the conversation he asked if we had found a church yet and invited us to attend church with them the next morning. As we followed them further and further, the road started to look strangely familiar. We turned off the main road at the same big white church we did two Sundays before but we did not stop at that church. We followed our neighbors' car and to our astonishment stopped in front of the church from the search engine, the one that we skipped two weeks earlier! God communicated through the search engine.

The message that Sunday spoke so clearly about what was relevant to us at the time. After church my wife and I went for lunch. We were still a little shaken up.

The message that Sunday was about Abraham and Sarah and how the Father made a promise to Abraham that he would have a child. Abraham had to wait for *twenty five* years and in time he decided to take matters into his own hands. Ishmael was born to his wife's maidservant. The consequences of that action had lasting repercussions. The Father was true to His Word and gave Abraham a son with Sarah and he became the father of many nations as promised. The moral of the story is that we should not take matters into our own hands if God has clearly given us an instruction. We should put our trust in Him.

We believed that when God wanted to bless us with children He was well capable of doing so and we should not pursue medical help to achieve this goal in an artificial way. Many times this was very hard for us, but the Lord always sent someone our way to convince us otherwise whenever we considered placing this matter in human hands. (The Lord's instruction applied to us personally and I do not suggest that people should not seek medical help in general.)

Eighteen months before we left Scotland my wife convinced me however to put our names on the waiting list for artificial insemination. Like Gideon we changed our prayer to be the opposite of what it was. We asked God to block our efforts if it was not in line with His plan.

> Then Gideon said to God, "Let not your anger burn against me; let me speak just once more. Please let me test just once more with the fleece. Please let it be dry on the fleece only, and on all the ground let there be dew."
>
> — Judges 6:39

Months went by without us being contacted. It so happened, that the notice with the counselor's appointment date was delivered while we were in Texas for the house-hunting trip.

The appointment was scheduled for the last Friday that I would be in Scotland and meant that there was no time to pursue the matter if we kept the relocation schedule. God did confirm that we should proceed with the relocation as planned only a few weeks before. After waiting for more than a year the timing could not be more inconvenient.

Some good news was presented to us during the appointment. The most recent tests showed marked improvement in our chances to be successful. We had spent many hours in prayer regarding the matter and for us the test results was a sign that God heard our prayers.

It is an emotional matter for any couple and even after the 'good news' we still struggled with the fact that we had 'missed our chance'. Truthfully, we wondered what the Lord was doing. Why arrange the appointment if we would be unavailable for treatment? At the same time we suppressed and hid our emotions very deep inside. The clock was ticking.

For us personally, the sermon in Houston a few months after the appointment, was a confirmation that we needed to leave this matter with the Father, even if it seemed that He had forgotten about us. God knew our internal struggle, reached out to us, and provided clarification - we were not victims of circumstance.

We did not know whether the Lord had delayed our attendance or had delayed the message to that Sunday. One thing was certain, God had it all planned out and was capable of executing His plan dynamically. He was determined not to leave us in the dark.

Because the Word from the Lord was so specific we did not know whether we only needed to be at that church, on that specific Sunday, or if this was our new church home. After a few more weeks of attendance and prayer time we decided that this would be our church. The pastor and his wife gave us many opportunities to minister on a Sunday and also lead the prayer ministry.

Pastoring the church was not their fulltime jobs and we felt privileged to be able to help out. The Lord blessed us with meeting some wonderful people including our best friends in the US (also a God appointment).

Approximately four years later we felt that our season with the church was over and that the Lord was leading us elsewhere. This time around we hoped that our next church would be closer to our home.

It was 11 p.m. on a Saturday evening. We were ready to switch off the light when I said to my wife, "Let's ask the Lord to lead us to where we should go and not waste time. He did it before, He will do it again."

We had a couple of churches in mind for the next day, one of which was even further away than the church we attended at first. From the sermons we listened to online, this church seemed to be Spirit-filled and Bible-based.

We prayed, "Dear Lord, please show us the church you want us to go to next. We will go where you want us and we know that you showed us before. Show us again. Amen." We switched off the light and in faith expected the Lord to provide an answer by the next day.

The next morning there was no 'protocol communication', but I felt we needed to go to the distant church that appeared to be Spirit-filled. My wife suggested that she could send a text message to the neighbor and find out if they wanted to come with us. They had moved to a church closer to their house but did not feel quite at home there. It appeared that this would be a great idea and the polite thing to do, but I asked my wife not to contact the neighbor.

I did not want our first impression of the church to be influenced by anybody else, so I suggested that we could ask them the next time.

We followed the Holy Spirit's lead and headed off to church on our own. The worship service was wonderful and reminded us of the worship sessions we experienced at the church back in Scotland. Later we found out that the worship leader was from Scotland originally. The message that was delivered by the pastor was very engaging, down to earth and real. We felt the Holy Spirit's presence in the service and checked most of the boxes that were important to us.

Once the service ended we sat for a moment processing what we experienced. "I think this could be our church", we agreed in unison. Smiling, we acknowledged that we needed confirmation even though we were pretty excited.

We did not want to make an emotional decision. Even though the prompting by the Holy Spirit is critically important, we never assume that we are flawless in hearing from the Lord. I believe God honors a sincere heart.

Just as we were about to stand up, a hand tapped me on the shoulder. I expected it to be one of the church members ready to welcome us and turned around. Much to my surprise, we were greeted by our neighbors!

Without us communicating our plans, they decided to attend this church (recommended to them several years earlier) on the same morning. In Houston, with many different church options, the likelihood of attending the same church without any communication is highly unlikely. Not only did the Lord provide another confirmation, but He did so in an unmistakable way, with the same people He used to confirm our first church in Houston.

Prayer is important to us and we decided to go to the prayer meeting on the Tuesday night. We were greeted by a small group of prayer warriors along with the pastor. Knowing that the prayer was an active part of the church and important to the pastor further confirmed our choice. We found our second church in Houston. God was making new connections and exposing us to new experiences to mold the miry clay.

The Lord can use us anywhere. It is better though to be in the center of God's plan. God's will is often uncomfortable to our human nature but spiritually an exhilarating and fulfilling place to be. The true presence of God tends to minimize any external influences that the natural environment brings.

~~~~~~

In Scotland we lived maybe ten minutes and a few miles away from work. Everything was in close proximity.

Settling in Houston, we were stunned by the distances we were required to travel because we lived on the outskirts. The time arrived when we needed to purchase another vehicle. Most of the vehicles on the road were foreign to us. We could not believe how different the cars were from those in Europe, both in look and size. We believed that a long-term view was the best approach, regardless of how many years we would be in the United States.

We did not have the money to spend on an expensive car at the time. A fuel-efficient and reliable sedan, that could carry four or five people for when we had visitors from overseas, summed up the requirements. It had to be a pre-owned car to minimize depreciation. To be upfront, most of the vehicles in America really looked ugly to us. Of course as time went by we started to think the European cars looked bland.

The car that stood out for us, a good size vehicle, was the Honda Accord. Research indicated that it was a very dependable vehicle. We thought it would be too expensive for our budget and that we needed to set our sights somewhat lower. We wanted to make sure we acquired what we needed and what we could afford and not necessarily what we wanted.

One day, returning from the store, a Honda Accord passed us initiating the discussion again. We needed discernment and decided to pray about the matter just there and then. "Lord, you have shown and provided for us so many times before. We want to do the right thing. We really like this model of car but are not sure if we should pursue it. Please help us to find the right car."

The Lord answered quickly and in a spectacular way. Seconds later as we emerged on the other side of the freeway, we were presented with our answer. We couldn't miss the shiny blue Honda Accord on a raised ramp at the dealership. God's hand was evident, so we decided to investigate and continued to the dealership owned by another manufacturer.

Buying a car and especially a pre-owned car can be daunting. Nobody wants to face the salesman and the sometimes strong-arm sales tactics. This time however we were blessed with a kind salesman who really wanted to help us. As our relationship progressed, my suspicions diminished.

The only problem with the car, which could cause us not to consider it any more, was the fact that the previous owner was a smoker and the car smelled very strongly of smoke. The salesman ensured us that this would not be a problem and they had a fix for that. He called it "the smoke bomb." Again I was a little skeptic.

The salesman's office was stacked with salesman of the year

awards but more importantly it was clear that he was a committed Christian. We ended up talking mostly about church and faith related matters. This was the most pleasant car buying experience I ever had.

At the time of purchase we had no idea what my wife would be doing several years later. She required a spacious, fuel-efficient vehicle and the Honda Accord was perfectly suited to the job. God knew what was ahead of us and when we asked for His guidance, He answered! The car was a good buy for us, and a great blessing from the Lord.

Why would the Lord communicate to us about buying a car? His Word is clear - if we ask according to His will He will answer, even if it is about a car.

> And this is the confidence that we have toward him, that if we ask anything according to his will he hears us. And if we know that he hears us in whatever we ask, we know that we have the requests that we have asked of him.
>
> — 1 John 5:14-15

God is willing to be part of every aspect of our lives. Communicate with Him and share your life with the One who has given His life for you.

The steadfast love of the Lord never ceases; his mercies never come to an end; they are new every morning; great is your faithfulness.

—Lamentations 3:22-23

12

EMERGENCY RESPONSE

Even though we may face some very tough opposition and very trying times in our lives, there is no question that God looks after those who are in the right standing with Him.

> For the eyes of the Lord run to and fro throughout the whole earth, to give strong support to those whose heart is blameless toward him...
>
> —2 Chronicles 16:9

Blameless does not mean without sin. That would be impossible to fully achieve while on earth. I believe it simply means a heart that is sincerely focused on the Lord, His commandments, purposes and objectives as the primary priority in life. It is the desire of the heart to sacrificially serve God with an attitude of thanksgiving. In simpler terms, loving the Lord and doing what He asks of us with a joyful heart.

Many books have been written about prayer and about fasting, two very important subjects. Topics include how to pray, the importance of spiritual warfare, the importance of a relentless commitment, praying without ceasing, to pray in faith, and to use our Kingdom authority. These are all critical spiritual truths and skills to apply in regard to a circumstance or purpose in our lives.

What about those circumstances that we are unaware of that impact our lives; events and crisis situations that happen without prior warning?

God will support us but He can also supernaturally inform and guide us regarding current or future events. He knows the end from the beginning. He created all things including time, which does not restrict His actions.

This may be a difficult concept to grasp. In an effort to practically explain this topic, I will use the analogy of a film director. When producing a movie the director is aware of all the characters and the storyline. During the filming process and also afterwards during the editing process, the movie is often adapted or changed. Changes can occur because of input from the actors, writers and other contributors. Sometimes alternative endings are filmed, the result of different storylines depending on the actions or decisions of the characters in the movie. Although the main storyline remains, the subplots often change to bring about the final result. Scenes from the movie may be cut during the editing process because they failed to contribute to the storyline or fit within the allotted time. Characters from those scenes may be replaced by others in alternative scenes. Even though the film follows a sequential storyline, the director may choose to film any scene at any time. Scenes from the end of the movie may be filmed at the beginning of the filming process and vice versa. The director does not have to follow the sequence of scenes because he is aware of all the scenes in the movie and how they fit together. The director is not restricted by the same constraints as the characters participating in the movie. The journeys of the characters are captured on the tape or disc but the director is able to hold the movie in his hands. The director exists outside the timeline of the movie.

God is able to alert us in the present (sometimes in our spirit) of events in the future so we can be part of changing the outcome. The Holy Spirit helps us to engage the matter in the spiritual realm (the operating system). Believers in Jesus are heirs of the Kingdom of God and the Holy Spirit guides us to assert our authority.

We should never limit God's work in our lives to the boundaries of our own intellect. This results in a lack of faith. Practically we always need to be ready to do what God asks of us.

God is sovereign and does not always call on us or make matters work out the way we prefer. Sometimes the final outcome of events is a mystery to us. We cannot understand it all. What we can do however, is to position ourselves in the best possible way to function in God's Kingdom and receive His blessing.

Always keep in mind that God loves you. We find ourselves in the middle of an age old battle between good and evil. We are only aware of what is revealed to us through the Bible or the Holy Spirit.

Far too often crises or tragedies are attributed to God's will. The Father promises good things over and over in the Bible to those who love Him. So why do so many Christians always point the finger at the Father first when in torment, believing it is His will? The Bible is full of promises of protection by the Father against many challenges and dangers in our lives if we abide in Him. The

Son of God died for us on a cross through great suffering. Why would the same God dish out tragedy all the time?

One has to believe that God's intentions are noble and that He has our best interest at heart. This assurance is critical for one to remain standing and to operate in God's Kingdom, when the hatred and tremendous violence of the enemy is released against you. Satan hates man with a passion and wants nothing less than to destroy the crown of God's creation.

Anything that is from the Father is ultimately for our good. Nothing that is evil is from the Father. If what we face does not align with the Word of God, we need to fight it with all we have in prayer and worship. Only then can we be sure that the final outcome is the best the Lord has in store for us. If we don't fight, we will never know if we contributed to defeat because of our own failure to position ourselves for victory.

~~~~~~

My wife and I experienced strong interventions from the Lord during our time in Scotland, after my wife gave up her secular job to serve at the church. Living abroad, the most challenging aspect was missing our families. This was especially true for my wife. It was very hard for her not to be there to support or celebrate with her family depending on the circumstances in their lives. If she kept her secular job, she would have been able to go home and see the family more often. The Lord honored her commitment to serve Him.

One morning my wife was commuting to church when she heard the audible sound of an ambulance approaching. She looked around immediately to see if she should move out of the way, but could not see an ambulance. "That was weird", she thought. There was no question that she heard an ambulance approaching.

My wife's heart responded to the prompting of the Holy Spirit and she started to pray for the incident, and then prayed for the family of the person involved since the sound of the ambulance did not subside. She continued to pray that God will save the life of the person in the ambulance. The audible sound stopped as soon as she pleaded for the unknown patient's life. My wife did not know who she was praying for, but God did.

> "Because he loves me," says the Lord, "I will rescue him; I will protect him, for he acknowledges my name. He will call on me, and I will answer him; I will be with him in trouble, I will deliver him and honor him. With long life I will satisfy him and show him my salvation."
>
> —Psalm 91:14-16

One week later my wife's father crashed in his light aircraft on takeoff at a small airfield. He suffered severe burns to parts of his body and his neck was broken. The condition of his neck was unknown to the men who bravely pulled him out of the burning wreckage and dragged his body over an uneven grassy field to safety.

When the paramedics arrived and established my father-in-law's condition, he was immediately taken to a local hospital. After he was stabilized an ambulance transported him to a hospital in a city two hours away.

At the time we were with friends in Ireland for Christmas. My wife strongly felt that she needed to phone home on Christmas Eve (we would typically phone on Christmas Day). During the phone call the Holy Spirit prompted her to ask some questions and from the answers she knew something was wrong. At my wife's insistence, her family shared the news that my father-in-law had just been in an accident and that his condition was very serious. Knowing that God prepared the way one week in advance, we started to pray in agreement that his life will be spared. All the surgeries that were required went well and my father-in-law survived a horrendous accident. What a loving God we serve who honors His servants.

That Christmas we celebrated a Savior that was born thousands of years ago, but more importantly who's impact on our lives are eternal.

A few years later my wife was at a restaurant with fellow Christian women when she physically felt her heart racing. Consulting with the Holy Spirit she knew she had to pray for someone's heart to be healed. The next morning she phoned her aunt in South Africa. God showed His mighty intervention once again! My mother-in-law's heart started racing that very night my wife prayed and the only way to stop the acceleration was for doctors to stop the heart and start it again. I believe that once more the Lord honored my wife.

After we joined the prayer ministry and pursued ways to be involved more directly in the Lord's work in Houston, unexpected things started to happen. This was a clear indication that we were heading in the right direction because Satan didn't like it.

On one occasion my wife was on her way to an appointment when she rear-ended a SUV with her car at low speed. Even at that low speed a lot of damage could have been done because the SUV's rear fender is higher than the front fender of a normal car. Fortunately the impact was absorbed by the hood which crumbled as designed.

This was our first accident in all the years we had been together. The fact that the accident was in the United States added to my wife's shock and stress because the United States is renowned for lawsuits about seemingly trivial matters.

My wife's neck and shoulders were sore but she did not suffer any major injury. In the confusion the first thing she thought of was to phone the realtor to cancel the appointment. As God arranged it, the realtor was close by and immediately came to my wife's aid. The fact that the realtor knew the police officer that appeared on the scene, and assisted my wife through the process while I was on my way, was a real blessing. I was in the middle of a stressful business meeting when my wife phoned me, but the Lord gave me great peace of mind. I can be a reactive person when confronted with surprises, but an extreme calm came over me. I just knew everything would be alright.

The car showed significant damage but did not have to be written off and could be repaired. We did not get sued at the time but a year later after I had left my long time career Satan used the incident to try and instill fear. We received a letter from our insurance company indicating that the other party had put in a big insurance claim because of the incident.

Satan's plan came to nothing. In fact, the Lord used the incident for good only a few weeks after it happened. A friend of ours came to visit and the rental car that was allocated to us by the insurance company was put to good use.

~~~~~~

Our Heavenly Father, the Creator of all things, is intricately involved in our lives. Why would He be, if the end of our existence was when we passed away? It only makes sense because He is building an eternal relationship, preparing us to live in His Kingdom forever.

At times the only way we can experience peace is through the Holy Spirit imparting the peace of the Lord within us. Lasting peace however comes from the assurance that God is with us. Not just head knowledge, but a deep seated belief in our hearts, because we know that we are in a relationship with Him.

Yes, we are set free by grace alone, but faith without works is dead. How do we show we truly love our spouses and our children? How are lasting marriages characterized? By deeds that confirm the words of love and commitment.

Even though the Lord loves us unconditionally, actions have consequences. Under spiritual law, protection and blessings result from obedience. Rebellion leads to adverse consequences. Satan, the accuser, is ready to take advantage of any habitual sin or resentment that we harbor. It is important that we manage our lives correctly.

Now this is the commandment - the statutes and the rules - that the Lord your God commanded me to teach you, that you may do them in the land to which you are going over, to possess it, that you may fear the Lord your God, you and your son and your son's son, by keeping all his statutes and his commandments, which I command you, all the days of your life, and that your days may be long. Hear therefore, O Israel, and be careful to do them, that it may go well with you...

—Deuteronomy 6: 1-3

There is no question that I have experienced God's involvement and protection when my life has been the purest and most aligned with God's Word. At times when I strayed, I experienced more strife, discontentment and what seemed like silence from God.

God is able, and through the Holy Spirit communicates situations beyond our realm of awareness to us. All we need to do is to be in a position to receive His help.

It is very important that friends and family pray for each other all the time. Each prayer is stored in vessels in heaven and poured out at the appropriate time to attend to the unforeseen circumstances in our lives.

My mother has made it a priority to pray for all her children continuously especially after we left home. I call it, "Requesting air support." Only when we get to heaven will we know how those prayers impacted our lives, but from the interventions that we have experienced, I can imagine quite extensively.

We are not meant to walk this road alone. Let's help each other to complete the journey.

The Lord reigns, let the earth rejoice; let the many coastlands be glad! Clouds and thick darkness are all around him; righteousness and justice are the foundation of his throne. Fire goes before him and burns up his adversaries all around. His lightnings light up the world; the earth sees and trembles. The mountains melt like wax before the Lord, before the Lord of all the earth. The heavens proclaim his righteousness, and all the peoples see his glory. All worshipers of images are put to shame, who make their boast in worthless idols; worship him, all you gods!

—Psalm 97:1-7

13

NEXUS

Nexus – A connection or relationship between people or things

Nothing that God does, ever, is random or on impulse. Our Father in heaven is passionate about His creation but He is calculated in His actions; slow to anger, quick in mercy. He is the most incredible director. God is the source of all things and nothing in the lives of those whom fear Him go unnoticed and unmanaged. Not a single life of any of the multitude that serves Him is without a plan and an intended purpose.

Everything in our lives, even the self-inflicted sorrows is used by the conductor. All of our experiences are woven together in a concert of the lowest lows to the highest highs; from the up tempo lightness of pure joy to the down tempo weight of consciousness.

Every relationship, assignment and every event shapes us towards the point where we are ready for all that God has created us to be. The outcome is spectacular if we choose to participate.

When I was younger, I lived life to the maximum. The objective was always the next destination. Life was divided in modular periods of time, each with a distinct beginning and end. Later on I began to notice the continuous hand of God in my life through all stages. Partly because of the natural change due to aging and partly because of the years of processing information, identifying and defining relationships as part of my career.

Although my life could be broken down in distinct periods, every experience and influence was purposed to equip me and formed a multidimensional nexus. An intricate support network was being developed to continuously bring me closer to the point of optimization. Optimized to live according to the purposes the Lord had in mind for me when I was still in the womb. Molded to live my dream even if I never realized what it was. I was instinctively drawn to it by the desire the Lord placed in my spirit the day I was created.

Our dreams provide a window into our purpose if our hearts are aligned with God's Word and we are truly honest with ourselves. The most difficult part is to understand what our dreams are. The constant bombardment and guidance by the expectations of the world, our families and friends typically nudges us onto a path far removed from the one defined by the Lord's roadmap.

The only way to find God's path is to constantly communicate with the Lord, learning to hear His voice and then be willing to take the risk of being obedient. It does not happen by being passive but requires resolve. From my perspective, contrary to the theory of evolution, nothing changes by itself into a complex intelligent entity without being driven by design and intent. I have determined that it is better to act than to wait.

At some point in your life, if you take the time to think about the journey you have been on and the moments or opportunities of contact you had with God and people, the Almighty will confront you. He will come to you and maybe He has come to you already with an offer, "Here is your mission, if you choose to take it on. I have already prepared you." It could be a completely new direction or it could be finally stepping up to spiritually lead or serve in your household, circle of friends or community to the glory of God. Yesterday does not exist and tomorrow is boundless if you are redeemed by Jesus Christ, who sits at the right hand of the Father.

...And if it is evil in your eyes to serve the Lord, choose this day whom you will serve, whether the gods your fathers served in the region beyond the River, or the gods of the Amorites in whose land you dwell. But as for me and my house, we will serve the Lord.

—Joshua 24:15

BLESSING

The Lord really blessed us from the start in Houston Texas. I spent three and a half years working on a mega project. The scope and complexity of the project was enormous, especially in the discipline I was responsible for. Being about ten years younger than the other Lead Engineers in the core team, the pressure was on to prove I was capable of doing the job.

Inside I knew that I would work hard and give it my best. These sizable projects however are larger than our own abilities and require a large team to complete successfully. Even with a large team and strict procedures, the chance of something being overlooked or missed at some point is pretty good. Because of the scale of the project, a single miss could have a massive impact, as every design decision is multiplied a multitude of times.

In the midst of the storm I spent hours responding to e-mails, writing and reviewing design documents and interfacing with multiple customers and vendors. I soon came to the realization that there was no way I would be successful in the position without God's backing. From the start I submitted to the Lord. I frequently reconfirmed the same statement, "Lord, I depend on you to cover my back for the matters that I have no control over and the things that I miss. I trust in you to save me from disastrous mistakes. I will continue to do my utter best to fulfill my role and proceed with excellence to bring You glory. I will deal with all people, in all situations, in a way that is pleasing to you. Amen"

The Lord shows His uncompromising support for His people regardless of their weakness and temporary state of mind. When we move in the direction purposed by the Father, He typically does not take us out of our circumstances, but rather confirms that He is with us in the fire.

> But he said to me, "My grace is sufficient for you, for my power is made perfect in weakness."
>
> —2 Corinthians 12:9

Not only did I get the chance to work with some great people during my time with the project, but I was also able to speak into people's lives and support them on a human level.

The Lord repeatedly showed His involvement, leaving His calling card along the way, reassuring me that I was on the right path. I was assigned to a desk on floor *seven* when I arrived at the Houston office, while the rest of the team was located on another floor. A few weeks later I had to move down to another floor together with the team. Our home in Scotland was still not sold and only days were left before my wife would have to depart for Texas. If you recall, I prayed and worshipped for a week before the house was sold in the last hours my wife was in Scotland. During the week that I prayed, the whole core team was moved back up to the *seventh* floor, where we remained for several months before the project kicked into full gear and a larger space was required for the team.

The most time-consuming part of the job was to produce extensive design specifications and other design documents. These documents evolved as the project continued and were constantly updated and had to be very accurate as they were at the center of both the design and commercial agreements. Besides being technically accurate, the correct wording needed to be used to ensure that no ambiguity existed.

On a number of occasions, when I had to justify or motivate a design or action, I would put a number of structured points together. While thinking it over during a coffee break a critical point would come to mind. In those instances my list of points would end up being a total of *seven, seven*teen or another number containing a *seven*. Those points typically turned out to be what swung the pendulum.

God's calling card on these occasions, gave me the internal peace to argue the point with conviction. Not because I wanted to be right, but because it would be the best solution for the project from my perspective.

Did I make mistakes? Sure. All the glory goes to God for managing my mistakes.

DECOUPLING

After about three and a half years the design work was pretty much done and the individual parts of the project implementation were well on their way. The next phase was scheduled to be executed in the country where the plant was being constructed.

The Lord had pressed on my heart soon after we arrived in the US that we should apply for permanent residence. At the time I did not think much of it. When the project moved into the next phase, I felt the Lord prompting me again to pursue permanent residence and not to waste time. To apply I would need the help from my employer. I did not want to rock the boat. It could be easily perceived that I had imminent plans to leave the company, plans that I did not have at the time. I had worked for the company for sixteen years and was in a position where I could exert some influence and deploy my ideas corporately. Still God would not relent.

The Holy Spirit injected a chapter of scripture into my thoughts one Sunday morning during prayer time before church.

Remember also your Creator in the days of your youth, before the evil days come and the years draw near of which you will say, "I have no pleasure in them"

—Ecclesiastes 12:1

For most of my adult life, I was either involved in church activities or personally ministering to people. I always felt that one day my wife and I would spend more time in ministry as a main purpose and not a secondary activity, the emphasis being on, 'one day'.

I frequently found myself in an internal struggle, 'one day' always seemed in the distance and impossible to attain in the short-term. That Sunday morning I felt the Lord communicated to me, "I don't want you to wait until your energy and drive is spent. Why not focus more on me now? "

I pondered and wrestled with this for a while and although my heart was receptive, my mind saw obstacles. Besides, my career was approaching a summit where I would be happy to remain for a while. I did not immediately put two and two together but the message was another node, another connection in the nexus of our journey. The Lord kept pressing the issue and Satan kept highlighting people that crossed my path and had struggled to complete the same process.

It came to a head and through prayer I decided that I had to proceed, if not for the sake of obedience, then for the sake of security for my family. A meeting was set up with my manager to discuss the subject. I had touched on the subject lightly before but this would be an all guns blazing effort and I was concerned about the possible fallout.

While driving to the office, about a mile away from work, I prayed to the Lord and placed the meeting in His hands. I was very nervous as this could be one of those moments that had a major impact on our personal futures. When I finished my prayer driving with my eyes open, I reached down to turn on the radio. The first words emanating from the sound system was a song phrase quoting a verse from the book of Romans,

If God is for us, who can be against us?

—Romans 8:31

It lifted my spirit as I was reminded that I had a divine sponsor for the meeting. The quote in itself would have been a great confirmation for me but God wasn't done. When I looked up my eyes met what looked like a giant cross levitating in midair. After my eyes adjusted to the light, I realized that it was a tow bar on the back of a vehicle recovery truck. Typically the metal beam structure that is used to tow vehicles is in a T-shape at a flat angle on the back of the truck while unused. On that day the structure in front of me was vertical at close to a ninety degree angle with the vertical beam extended above the T-bar to make the structure appear in the form of a Roman cross. Where the truck suddenly came from I don't know. There was nobody in front of me when I glanced down to switch on the radio.

I felt the presence of the Lord and immediately acknowledged His hand of provision. God spoke and instead of writing it off as coincidence, I recognized it for what it was. The Father communicated like only He can. The timing and relation of the events happening right at that time in that sequence and in seconds, was unmistakably God.

When I walked to the entrance of the office building there was a maintenance truck parked right next to the front door with a large number *seven* on its door.

The meeting with my manager, who I thought was just doing his job, got really heated and combative but in the end the process to obtain permanent residence was started. If I did not know the Lord was in it, I may have backed down during that meeting.

If you live in expectation of the Lord communicating in every situation, you enable yourself to recognize Him in any mosaic of signs or impressions on your soul and senses. That morning's confirmation by God is one of the engagements that I frequently think back to when I need strength to face a new challenge.

~~~~~~

For his invisible attributes, namely, his eternal power and divine nature have been clearly perceived, ever since the creation of the world, in the things that have been made. So they are without excuse.

—Romans 1:20

God is always communicating, encouraging and showing His hand in all things, big or small. All of creation testifies of the Lord, even to those who don't know Him. All systems and inventions that we create as humans require the creative power of God. Therefore God, the source, has power and authority over every living entity and manmade mechanism and may use it for His purposes when He desires to do so.

~~~~~~

Getting approval to go ahead with the application for permanent residence was not the end of the battle. After submitting an application for permanent residence, applicants were advised not to inquire about applications before six months have passed. After six months our applications were still at the initial status of "application received."

I phoned the contact number and the representative advised me that the applications were moved from the local area processing office to a main processing office in another state. I was also told that the process had started again, and I should wait another six months. The wind was taken from my sails. Memories of our move from Scotland and the struggle to sell the house came to mind and we wondered if, once again, we would face a lengthy battle to complete this act of obedience.

That same Thursday evening, once the dust had settled, we decided to take the matter to the Lord in prayer. In this case we felt the Lord instructed us to use our authority in Him and speak to the problem. We commanded the application to be completed. In our minds we set the expectation that it may take a few weeks and were at peace with that. To our surprise, when we fetched the mail the following Monday both our Green Cards where in the mail. The envelopes were posted the previous Friday. We were overjoyed and astounded.

~~~~~~

In every situation there is something to be learned. Not all battles are the same and what worked for one does not necessarily work for the next. Similarly, what did not work for a previous battle may work for the next one. Only God has a clear view of what is required for a breakthrough in the spiritual realm at any given time. Only through expecting, being sensitive and alert to the voice of the Lord can we proceed in the most effective and efficient way through the obstacles in our paths. God never changes, but we need to constantly change to renew our minds and our souls and maintain our faith.

Many people would describe their lives as boring, mundane and possibly hopeless because they base their future possibilities on past experiences. If we have that vision, it ultimately casts the living God in the same mold as a dead idol. We are unable to receive because we have tried once, failed and assumed the Lord is capable but not willing.

Although the good news of the Gospel is simple and what we need to do to experience a blessed life is clear, the Bible states that we will have trouble in this world.

Many believers choose not to read this part. Other believers only read this part and settle for a life of defeat. The truth is that we will face troubles but we are destined to overcome those troubles through God's power and bring glory to His name. God is more than a phrase in a fortune cookie. We need to shape up and engage at the level He created us to operate in.

Belief is required. Faith is not belief if it is not challenged to determine if the grace of God is alive in the faithful. To win these battles, to slay the Goliaths in our lives, is not always easy but the Lord promises us victory, He does not promise us that there will be no war. The question we ask should not be "Lord why?", but "Lord what do I need to do different next time to overcome?"

From my experience I can assure you that even if you fail numerous times, the Lord will not stop in His relentless support until you get it right. In this regard I am a living testimony.

If we love, obey and serve the Lord, we are blessed. It does not mean we will experience no troubles, it means that we are blessed even in those troubles because we have the assurance of intimacy with the living God. This is the place of everlasting contentment.

PREPARATION

The Lord allowed me to grow in different areas and set up His support network for me. God provided a new Christian friend in the workplace for the next part of the journey.

I was released from the project I worked on since arriving in the US and took on a more general role instead of being assigned to a specific project. I worked to promote engineering excellence and supervised a number of engineers as their functional manager. Part of the responsibility meant that I would engage early on and at a higher level with potential customers to determine solutions for upcoming projects and also work on proposals to meet their needs.

One of my first assignments was to work as part of a team interfacing with a global customer in the energy sector to improve design processes, in preparation for the next mega project.

The team built a great relationship with the customer and developed trust. It was a privilege for me to work with the highly talented individuals from all over the globe. It also allowed me to engage with senior management on a regular basis. It was a great opportunity to learn, retain the good and reject the bad.

After a number of months the team was asked to put together a proposal for the customer (in competition with other vendors) regarding an upcoming project.

At the same time one of my wife's best friends from her High School days in South Africa was planning to visit us in Houston. She would arrive from Britain and was planning to travel back to South Africa from Kansas City. This left an undefined travel gap between Houston and getting to Kansas City.

We looked forward to her visit. As usual, December was developing into a very busy month for my wife at work and on my side the prospects looked uncertain. We were waiting for the information from the customer to proceed with the project proposal. It would be possible to manage the project proposal work if we stayed in Houston. With our friend heading to Kansas City between Christmas and New Year, we were unsure of how we would manage.

We considered a twelve hour road trip, but the advanced weather predictions for December showed heavy snow along the road and hazardous driving conditions. As time drew closer to our friend's visit, work became more uncertain and plane tickets would just become more expensive. If we decided to drive, did we want to put the miles on our own vehicle or rent a car?

With so many changing variables we decided to ask the Lord for guidance. First request on the agenda was whether we would be able to drive in the conditions or whether we should rather fly. Driving would give us more flexibility to cater for uncertain work schedules but could be dangerous or not work out due to road conditions. If it was not for the fact that we wanted to attend the Christian conference with her, an alternative could have been to let our friend travel on her own.

It was a simple prayer, "Lord we really want to take our friend on this journey and meet up with so many believers. Can you please help us to know if we would be able to drive to Kansas City and whether it is the way we should go?" As soon as we concluded the prayer I decided to open up an online map application and determine the distance that we would have to travel. I entered Kansas City as the destination and took the effort to enter our exact home address as origin. As I hit the go button, I wondered why I did not just type the origin city name since a few miles were not going to make a big difference on such a long journey. My answer came immediately.

The map software displayed three possible routes with the highlighted or quickest route suggested being exactly *seven hundred and seventy seven* (777) miles. It turned out that this would be the distance to the conference facility which was located in the city center.

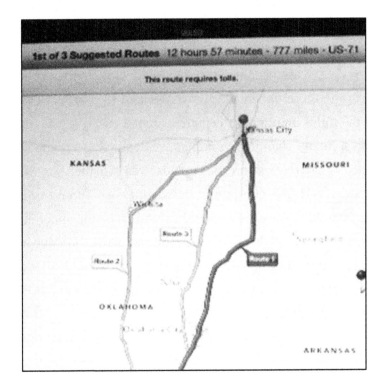

Kansas City Road Trip: "777"

A burst of excitement hit me and I jumped up blurting out, "We should go and we need to drive. The Lord said we will be safe and this is the way to go."

Right there and then we agreed that we were going on a road trip. We still needed to decide if we would put the miles on our own car or rent a car. We phoned a few rental places but there did not seem to be any real cost saving.

It was during this time that my wife was involved in the collision with the SUV. As part of the insurance support, we received a rental car to drive while our car was being repaired. The way it worked out, the repair company would only be able to finish the repair two days after we planned to return from Kansas City.

Not only did the Lord tell us to drive but He knew we would be in possession of a rental vehicle with low fuel consumption to take us to our destination and back. It never snowed while we were on the road. The Lord made everything work out for good. In addition, the information from the customer to prepare the proposal arrived very late. With all the uncertainty during that period and the way everything worked out, in even the smallest detail, was only enabled by the Lord's hand of grace.

It was at this Christian conference that God engaged with me to write about His majesty. At another time during the event, I received a verse that I felt was from God as an indication of what lay ahead in the following year. On our way back to Houston we stopped over for New Year's Eve to break the long trip in two. First thing the next morning I checked all the text messages and e-mails that came in with wishes for the New Year. One of the e-mail messages was from my new friend from work. He sent me a verse that he felt was for me. It was exactly the verse that I received at the conference. That verse turned out to be an accurate account of what transpired in the year that followed and wrapped up a special week of God's involvement.

After the proposal was submitted, the team had to clarify a number of items with the most important ones discussed during a number of meetings held with the customer.

I do not want to take anything away from the team that worked on the pursuit, but I would like to highlight what I believe was one of the pivotal points.

The technical leader from the customer's side had built up a good trust relationship with one of our main competitors over the years. Trust is something that takes a very long time to build. We had to compete with that trust relationship. The motto of our team was integrity and transparency without holding back the unique benefits of our solutions and level of commitment that we would provide to the customer. I believe we had better solutions for the magnitude and complexity of the project that was to be undertaken. I did not feel like the customer was convinced or trusted us completely.

One evening after many months of hard work, before a technical clarification meeting with the customer, I felt that instead of spending more time in preparation for the meeting, my friend and I should spend time in prayer. Something in my spirit told me that there were obstacles involved with this pursuit that could not be overcome by mere human skill and ability. Our prayer contained the words of two men that truly pursued the best interest for all, believing that our team would be part of the solution. The result was in the hands of God.

We prayed that the Holy Spirit would operate in each member of the team the following day. The prayer included the whole team regardless of their perception of God. We asked that the team would speak in one voice so that our work would be presented in the best possible way.

The team was confident going into the meeting. Besides the team, a senior manager also attended the meeting that day. Instead of starting on fire, we were dealt an unexpected blow in the first five minutes. The lead technical representative from the customer, visibly upset, implied that we could all go home. His comments were directed at the engineer (obviously disappointed) responsible for the presentation. Not the kind of start to the meeting that we prayed for! More often than not I have learned that when God steps in, there needs to be something for Him to do that is beyond our capabilities. It shows His strength and presence. The team rallied behind our colleague in peril and started speaking in one voice completing each other's sentences and thoughts from different perspectives. This incredible harmony of the engagement continued on all topics.

The rest of the meeting went well and at the end I felt embattled but satisfied. After the meeting my manager came into my office and said that he had heard from the senior manager that we handled the meeting incredibly well, addressing all topics with confidence and competency. The most impressive part was that we all spoke like we were the same person. He had never seen anything so dynamic being addressed so synchronized and aligned. The Lord honored two believers who decided that it was more important to seek the help of the Almighty than to trust in their own abilities.

God honors His relationship with us. How often do we not stumble in the same way that we stumble in our relationships on earth, by not spending the time? We read books and look for complex solutions when all that is required is acknowledging the Creator, the Designer, and spending the time to seek Him. Getting to know Him deeper and deeper with a sincere heart changes us through the power of the Holy Spirit. It does not consist of a ten step plan, only willingness and obedience.

For nothing will be impossible with God.

—Luke 1:37

The meeting also had personal significance. The senior manager that attended previously fulfilled the position (as part of his many responsibilities) that I accepted a few months earlier. For me this was a test to see if I had what it takes to fulfill the role. When I considered this specific position, it was a step of faith. The area of responsibility included Canada, North America and South America. In addition I would work on initiatives impacting the way we engineered globally.

All in all it was a daunting challenge. I would fulfill this role, along with functionally managing a team of engineers. The Lord knew that this was part of a larger plan on His timeline and I needed to pursue the function immediately. After some prayer I wandered down to the floor hosting my future office. It was closer to the people that reported to me.

It wasn't the *seventh* floor. The whole group was being moved to floor number three. For a moment I was reminded of the very stressful time I spent on the second floor when we just moved to the Texas office. It made me wonder if I was heading in the right direction, the direction that the Lord intended for me.

Up to that point I had received no specific communication from the Lord according to our agreed (in His mercy) protocols regarding the position. I only received general communication that indicated that I would soon utilize all the skills and abilities that I had acquired over the years.

All the offices in the building were numbered but typically the numbers were not to be found anywhere but on layout charts. When I walked up to my new space, I noticed that the office number was visible on the door frame. Somebody decided to print a small standard text label for the office which one would probably not notice if you were not looking. I also noticed the name of the person that occupied the office at that time posted on the wall outside the office.

I was stunned,

Office number..... *"3-16"*
First name of occupant (Spanish)..... *"Jesus"*

For God so loved the world, that he gave his only Son, that who-
ever believes in him should not perish but have eternal life.

—John 3:16

John 3:16 is one of the most well-known verses in the Bible. The Lord was in this new role! The method with which he confirmed the next part of my journey was unique. There was no way that a believer that was on the lookout for God to speak to Him, would miss this very obvious message from God. Then I started to wonder why God was so 'upfront'

He did not use our protocol but chose to emphasize the reason I had any business being in a relationship with the Father; His only begotten Son, who demonstrated the ultimate act of obedience by giving His life for sinners. What did this mean?

In time I found out that I was entering a new phase in my journey and soon God was going to request a step change from me.

During the last year at the company the Lord blessed me with many great interactions and experiences but the assignment He gave me to write about Him often came to mind. The Holy Spirit reminded me that the Lord very clearly said to me that if I chose to say "Yes", I would have to complete the task. If I did not intend to follow through, I should not promise anything to Him. The Lord's Word does not return void and neither should ours.

We live in a world of multi-tasking where the tools like computers, remote access and smart phones do not make our lives less hectic but overwhelmingly serve the interest of mammon. It is difficult to break free from its hold on our time.

IGNITION

One of my assignments in the final months involved writing a document with a highly educated and esteemed colleague in England. We had regular sessions in the morning US time which would be late afternoon or evening UK time. In between sessions we would write the portions of the document assigned to us in parallel. Some days we would spend some time visiting online and talking about other interests. I had the privilege to work with many good people in my career and I learned to appreciate the personal engagements.

One of the days that we needed a break from the task at hand, my colleague on his own accord started to talk about how he approached the books that he wrote outside of work. Facilitated by his doctorate degree, he writes manuals and text books used for teaching. The Holy Spirit reminded me of my assignment and I started asking my colleague about what software he used to write and publish the books. He went on to explain the whole process and what you need to do so that publishers can use the format of the books that you write without having to reformat. This saves on cost and allows for electronic publishing. Through this work partnership the Lord put me in a position to receive advice and nudged me forward in what He assigned me to do.

More and more tasks were put on my plate and I arrived home exhausted most evenings and spent weekends recovering or working to catch up. I took pride in my work and wanted to do a quality job. As the Bible instructs, we should do all things as onto the Lord. Even though I enjoyed my work, the most frustrating part was not being able to give every task my best effort. There just weren't enough hours in the day.

I was still very blessed and felt no real inclination to look for greener pastures because I knew it would probably be the same elsewhere. God however stirred something in me that made me consider not continuing my career until retirement age as planned. Any move would require risk and discomfort, so I basically put it on the back burner. The fact that I did not spend time writing however still bothered me.

We had planned a trip to South Africa to visit and help my parents move from their home of thirty four years to a retirement community in a city. The trip was planned *seven* months earlier without me knowing what my circumstances, the status of the major project pursuit or completion date of my folk's new home would be. My dad managed the home builders like he did a project when he was in the prime of his career. God blessed our faith and worked a completion that enabled them to move into the house as planned with only a day or two to spare.

During a lunch break at a burger place the week before we departed for South Africa, I found myself staring at the receipt with the order number *forty seven* in big bold letters at the top and transaction number *forty seven* at the bottom. It was a similar repetition as the previous time with *twenty seven*. This time the repetition was in the transaction number. It was my calling card, with a four in front. I had the same feeling in my spirit as before we visited our friends in California as I explained in the first chapter. I suspected that the number *forty seven* would be significant for the trip to South Africa and that the trip in itself would be important.

Order:"47" (777)

I was very excited and immediately phoned my wife. I love my wife dearly and without her I would not be a fraction of the man that I am. Her counsel and support has been more precious to me than what I could ever have dreamed to expect when we said "I do", so many years ago. It was important for me that she was included and validated my sanity as our journey continued.

Satan's continuous efforts to discourage would have been very tough to face alone. Both of us were stunned many times by the surgical communication by the Lord.

We departed to South Africa, not only with excitement to see our family but also with expectation to uncover where the Lord would lead us with 'forty seven'.

The last piece of the puzzle leading to a major life change would be put in place.

And that servant who knew his master's will but did not get ready or act according to his will, will receive a severe beating. But the one who did not know, and did what deserved a beating, will receive a light beating. Everyone to whom much was given, of him much will be required, and from him to whom they entrusted much, they will demand the more.

—Luke 12:47-48

14

FORTY SEVEN

Every instance of my journey where God provided clear instruction, He stretched me beyond what I thought was reasonable. In this 'unreasonable' territory where the boundaries of reason end, faith turns into a confident belief in His promises. God taught and prepared me for future assignments. The more times a rubber band is stretched, the more flexible it becomes, and the less resistance it presents to the one directing its shape.

We enjoyed a wonderful flight to South Africa. Due to the anticipation, we did not sleep much but still arrived in the GMT+2 time zone in fairly good shape. The flight from Atlanta Georgia arrived in Johannesburg at 5:30 p.m. We had travelled for almost twenty four hours in total and looked forward to a good night's sleep. The excitement of seeing the family after a long time pushed our bodies for a few hours more than they had intended to be without sleep.

A myriad of different conversations between different family members somehow intersected at times for common appreciation, only to diverge again into different avenues. At first the men and women discussed subjects of interest to their own domains, but eventually the discussions converged onto what was of importance to all - God.

It was a balancing act since everybody had plenty to share but not everybody could share at the same time. One had to keep the lid on until a genuine window of brief silence allowed for the initiation of a new subject.

We struggled to hold back on telling them about our view that the trip home was very significant and about everything that had been going on; everything that lead us to believe that a major change was imminent.

The women were in the kitchen and the men were browsing through some music videos when God initiated the conversation. A golden-oldie popped up onscreen at the same time that I considered sharing. I was convinced that the time had come for me to share with my brother. A large number *forty seven* was displayed in the bottom left hand corner of the screen enveloped by the fuzziness of the black and white video.

I blurted out that we needed to pause. The fuss drew the attention of the ladies in the kitchen who wanted to know what was going on. I explained that the number was significant and that I needed to share. To add to the moment of encounter, my wife noted, "I just started to talk about it in the kitchen!" God provided the opportunity and His approval and we started to share boldly.

A few weeks before our trip, my sister-in-law was very excited about a book that my brother wanted to give me as a present. On purpose, and with the intent to retain the surprise factor, I never asked what the book was about. God used my brother to bring me a specific message previously which added to the anticipation.

We spent the rest of the evening sharing intimately about God and what we had experienced. I explained the assignment to write and possibility make a career change. I concluded the expression of my feelings with the following statement, "I know that I can trust the Lord, this is not an issue. What I need to know without a doubt, is that it is part of God's plan for me? If I am sure, I will proceed regardless of the road that lies ahead because we will be fine if God is involved."

At the time I did not know how accurate, but ultimately prophetic those words would turn out to be. After praying together we went to bed late that night.

My brother gave me the book by Gunnar Olson, which is titled "Business Unlimited." It is a great book for any Christian, especially those active in the business world. It is Gunnar's life story and how he partnered with God to accomplish many feats, which include founding the International Christian Chamber of Commerce.

Even after traveling for about twenty four hours and with a seven hour time difference, I could not fall asleep that night. I eventually decided to get up early in the morning hours and started to read the book. I was fascinated from the beginning and just kept on reading at the desk lamp on the other end of the room, much to the annoyance of my wife who was pursuing a good night's sleep.

At around 4:00 a.m., I had made my way through to page forty six. The hair on my neck had risen, because it was like I was reading exactly what had been happening in our lives recently. I continued onto the next page. The words filled me with exhilaration mixed with a healthy fear, ignited by what I felt was a face to face meeting with the Lord.

161

Gunner's words read, *"Now, years later, I realize that God was giving me such clear encouragement because I needed to know that my resignation was somehow part of His plan for my life, just as the Israelites needed the cloud and the pillar of fire to guide them on their way to the Promised Land. There would be many obstacles ahead and difficulties to come, and I needed the deep security of knowing that I was in the hands of the Lord."*

His words echoed what I said earlier that evening. I considered the words for a minute or two. My eyes drifted to the bottom of the page. Page number *forty seven*! God confirmed the message that He had communicated.

At just after 4:00 a.m. in the morning I blurted out loud, "You've got to be kidding me!" I admit those were not the holiest of words, but I was in a state of awe of God's ability to orchestrate exactly what He needed to communicate to me. Maybe rather what I needed to hear.

He is the image of the invisible God, the firstborn of all creation. For by him all things were created, in heaven and on earth, visible and invisible, whether thrones or dominions or rulers or authorities—all things were created through him and for him. And he is before all things, and in him all things hold together

—Colossians 1:15-17

Gunnar's words proved to be a very accurate assessment of the journey that we faced. The onslaught of the enemy can become so fierce at times that only absolute faith in God enables us to continue with what we believe is His plan and not to take the easy way out.

When you are in the middle of an uncompromising battlefield

with the enemy, even admitting that your deepest belief was wrong is very tempting if it provides an exit. In those times only an absolute assurance that you are walking God's plan allow you to carry on. Communication is critically important.

The game was on so to speak. I had a three week visit with family to look forward to, but also three weeks of constant contemplation. The Lord spoke and now I had to decide if, how and when I would walk in obedience. Even though the chances were very slim, there was still the small possibility, that all of this just happened by coincidence. I was aware of the fact that I would have to make a compelling argument to justify this change as being a responsible course of action. God did not need me to justify Him, only to be obedient.

It would not make sense within the framework of the world. I would leave behind the security of employment in a job where I could use my experience gathered over the years. In exchange, I would pursue a new venture that I knew little about, with the only security being God's faithfulness in providing according to our needs.

Even though I had not come to a conclusion yet, I started to prepare our families by hinting that I was looking to make a change in career. Furthermore I shared that I was looking into a different line of work that would hopefully free up some time for me. I also informed them that I had started obtaining relevant education to gain some of the required knowledge.

During those three weeks I used every moment of spare time, of which there was little, to read the book my brother gave me and spend time with the Lord. It was a roller coaster ride but God is good and He knows the intent of our hearts even if our stomach may be spinning in retreat.

Throughout the trip God confirmed that this was His will. I will now share three of the most prominent communications from the Holy Spirit while in South Africa.

We were visiting my sister-in-law on their farm. Early one morning, I was heading back into the house to take a shower after I had finished my quiet time with the Lord in the front yard. My mind was processing what I had read that morning. Even though the book was very inspiring, it was clear that the road would probably not be very smooth. I thought of Paul's words about running the race of endurance,

> Therefore, since we are surrounded by so great a cloud of witnesses, let us also lay aside every weight, and sin which clings so closely, and let us run with endurance the race that is set before us, looking to Jesus, the founder and perfecter of our faith, who for the joy that was set before him endured the cross, despising the shame, and is seated at the right hand of the throne of God.
>
> —Hebrews 12:1

Searching for my wife and her sister, I entered into the doorway of the master bedroom where they said they would be. There was nobody in the room. When I turned to leave, my eyes were drawn to a framed photograph loosely placed on a chair. It was a photograph of my sister-in-law's daughter taking part in a cross country race with her face straining with effort. On her chest, she sported her entry number which ended in ... *"forty seven."*

Endurance Athlete: "…47"

Probably the most precious and memorable moment was when we were visiting my wife's parents on their farm. My wife and I joined my father and brother-in-law to do some work on a piece of land where livestock were grazing. One of the tasks on the agenda was to put out nutritional supplements (contained in bags) from the back of a pick-up truck.

My wife and I were mostly bystanders, but I did lend a hand whenever I could without being in the way. The supplements were dumped into a feeding trough and the cows gathered. They were attracted by the smell and pushed and shoved to find a spot around the trough. There wasn't enough space for all of them and positions were changed out, in an ongoing 'well mannered' rotation.

While this process continued, my mind wandered once again, thinking about the road ahead. My thoughts were suddenly interrupted when a young cow approached me and started to lick my arm. The typical reaction of cows to a stranger in the open field is to avoid close proximity, never mind licking your arm. The cow probably smelled supplement on my arm coming from the bags that I had handled but this kind of behavior was still very unusual. None of the other cows made an attempt to do the same.

Cow: "7"

Unbeknown to me, my wife was witnessing this incident, but more importantly, the mark on the cow's forehead. It was a white mark in the shape of a perfect *seven*. I walked over to my wife to share what I just experienced. Not only did she notice the cow licking me but also the mark. I went back to the cow to check the mark and confirmed that it was part of the cow's natural fur.

I asked my brother-in-law if the mark was natural or because of branding. He confirmed that it was natural. The timing and odd behavior together with the perfect *seven* shape on the forehead, could only have been arranged by God.

I was lounging in bed at my parent's new home one morning

towards the end of the trip. By then I was starting to consider when to resign my job. I felt that the Holy Spirit pressed "9-27" on my heart, which would be two weeks after I returned from vacation. It sounded reasonable and would give me time to progress a few things that I was working on to ensure a suitable handover. The still small voice inside me said, "No, 9-27 is not the day you resign, it will be your last day."

My immediate reaction was to quench this thought, because it did not sound practical or reasonable. I thought I needed to cool down for a minute and proceeded to open the messenger application on my phone to send a message specifically to my sister. I opened our message stream and my eyes noticed the status text at the top, "Last seen 9:27 a.m." (several hours earlier). You know, that you know, that you know is a phrase often used in Spirit-filled Christian circles. – I knew – the Lord's will was for "9-27" to be my last day, which meant that I had to resign the day after I returned to work.

There were only a few days left and my brother-in-law hosted a "braai" (BBQ/grill) which the whole of my wife's family attended. The men were outside next to the fire and the women mostly inside. I engaged in some deep discussions with my wife's uncle and also touched on some spiritual matters. He was under some strain at the time; he was called upon to help fellow farmers fight a fire more than a hundred kilometers away and needed to go back that evening to ensure that the fire did not resume.

At one point he shared a story from his youth that grabbed my interest. He was tasked to load bulls on a truck during the night and really struggled to get them onto the back of the truck. He explained how one can use a donkey to pull a bull to where you want him to go. He finished his story with, "After all, Jesus chose a donkey to ride into Jerusalem. We should not look down on a donkey, it is a strong animal." For me the story was fascinating and made an impression.

The time to travel back to Texas came all too quickly. We boarded the plane and found our seats for what I considered a time bubble in between states before we had to face real life again.

After the plane took off I continued reading "Business Unlimited." This time I came across a spiritual analogy which matched the story about the donkey told by my wife's uncle almost exactly. The Lord was adding another piece to the puzzle and gave me some indication of how a mere donkey, like mankind probably seems in the presence of the Lord, could be useful when guided by the Spirit of the Lord and overcome a seemingly superior force.

Back home in Texas, I knew that the primary trap that I needed to avoid was to give Satan a chance to foster doubt in my mind. I sent a meeting invite to my manager the first day (Thursday) that I was back in the office. The intent of the meeting was to catch up and possibly talk about my future plans. You probably noticed that I mentioned "possibly." The Gideon inside of me was wrestling with my spirit.

It was mid-afternoon and I struggled to get away from the notion that I needed to hand in my notice. I felt it was imminent. "Lord, you can communicate in very direct ways. If the sense in my spirit is correct and I need to resign, please send me somebody that I don't know to give me a word." In truth, I asked God to ignite the altar that I had soaked with water.

I thought the Lord needed some time. I also had an arrangement with my manager, that we would not give each other bad news on a Friday if it could wait until the Monday. Most of the time one could not do anything about it until the next week anyway. Why spoil somebody's weekend with bad news? I changed the meeting invite to Monday.

My wife describes me as someone who is not very approachable to strangers because my face generally seems preoccupied. I have to admit that this is true. I have been the cause of much amusement at times, when my mind would drift away during group conversations or at dinner and people would make fun of me, by talking about me and saying silly things without me having a clue of what was happening.

That Thursday afternoon I drove home and stopped at the gas station. I leaned against the side of the car while I waited and my mind went into overdrive, thinking about various things. There was a SUV parked on the other side of the pump. A boy wandered across the separation, chasing a balloon that had drifted to the space behind my vehicle. His face was so joyful and he smiled at me as he grabbed the strings attached to the balloon and ventured back to the other side. The joy on the boy's face made an impression on me.

The next thing I knew, a lady which I presumed to be his mother, approached me from behind the pump. "Sir", she said with a Caribbean accent as I admittedly gave her a, "Leave me alone, I have a lot on my mind" look.

"Sir", she repeated, "Are you a Christian?" She continued, "The Lord is great..." and spent about a minute declaring and giving praise to the attributes of God's character.

Looking me straight in the eye, the woman paused and said, "It is good to hear and know the Word of the Lord and His teachings. However, we should not only listen but act on His Words!" A little bewildered about the engagement I responded, "I agree."

The woman turned around, got back into her vehicle with her

boy and drove off without saying another word.

I was used to people that give words of knowledge from the Lord in church circles, but never before had a complete stranger approached me in public like this.

It was only when I sat down in the driver's seat that I remembered my prayer to God just a few hours earlier. The fear of the Lord hit me like a ton of bricks. "…Everyone to whom much was given, of him much will be required", suddenly carried a lot more weight. Sometimes we take the incredible privilege of a relationship with God for granted. It came at the ultimate price, one life for another - Jesus Christ.

On the Monday afternoon I spoke to my manager unofficially and told him that I would resign the next day, that my mind was made up and that I would like my last day to be "9-27", just under the customary two week notice period. After speaking to his manager he confirmed that it was agreed. The remaining days in the office was emotional but with the Lord's blessing I left on good terms with the company.

~~~~~~

God continued to present His calling card in the weeks and months to come when I needed it.

One occasion was when I had to acquire a new cellphone. While the sales person was busy entering my details in his tablet computer, I stopped myself from asking for a phone number that ended in forty seven. I wanted it as a reminder of that day, a monument in remembrance, not out of superstition.

The system selected a random number for my phone. My wife wrote it down while I attended to another matter. She displayed a radiant smile and said *"forty seven."* I was not amused, because I thought she was pulling my leg, and under the circumstances it was no laughing matter for me. I looked at the number and had to apologize; the number indeed ended in *"forty seven!"*

Five months after I left my long time career, I was working hard to build a new life. We were due to attend the wedding of one of our youth leaders from Scotland in Virginia, USA. At the time, the only way that we could afford to go was to drive from Texas. The timing was inconvenient and meant that we would lose a few productive working days. I was still uneasy about taking the trip right up to the point when we collected the fuel-efficient rental car.

The assistant at the rental car agency showed us two vehicles. One had a spacious interior with the necessary USB ports and interfaces that we would need for our electronic devices and to work while on the road. The other vehicle had a spacious trunk and lower fuel consumption, which we needed, but it looked very basic inside. I could see only a single analog audio port for connecting a device.

It seemed to be a choice between gadgets (required for our tech devices) and fit for purpose. The Holy Spirit's still small voice inside made me look at the serial number located on the windshield of the 'mundane' choice. It ended in "27." I was amazed with God's confirmation, "I support this trip."

To make sure all the serial numbers are not the same, I checked the other vehicle and discovered the serial number ended in "47"! Now I knew there was no doubt that God was involved. But what did it mean?

Both numbers were significant to me. I recalled that the numeral two in the Bible relates to discernment, witness and testimony and the number four with earth, rule, reign, kingdoms and creation. I decided that twenty seven was more important to me.

We managed to fit our entire luggage in the compact car and set off on a long drive. To my surprise I discovered that all the ports and the functions that were obviously available in the other car with its gadgets were also available in the one we picked. It was only hidden. All and all it was the better choice, but we could not 'see' it at the agency office.

God blessed us during the journey, seeing beautiful places and experiencing the splendor of God's creation. The number "27" kept repeating in addresses, site numbers, the car in front of ours on a ferryboat we chose on an alternative route etc. God decided we needed a break.

Ferryboat: "27"

The highlight was when we returned the rental car. I was handed the final receipt and noticed that we drove exactly three thousand eight hundred and "47"miles I did not exclaim out loud, "Are you kidding me!", but my spirit did! How intricately detailed is our King!

```
VEHICLE            927 ◄━━
LICENSE     _      937◄━
FUEL    FULL        8 /8 OUT
MILEAGE IN       6165
MILEAGE OUT      2318
MILES DRIVEN     3847 ◄━━
CDPXXXXXXX
```

Rental Car: "27", "47", "777"

One day when I needed encouragement to know that God would help me out of a mess I got myself into, a bright orange truck appeared. It announced itself in front of my home office window with the noise from its airbrakes. Painted on the side of the truck were the words, "GOD IS" and the number "7"

Truck: "7"

Everything was created and revolves around God and is under His authority. God will use His authority to reach out to you.

Almighty God, Loving Father, Selfless Savior, Intimate Counselor – Ever Present Communicator.

"I, wisdom, dwell with prudence, and I find knowledge and discretion."

—Proverbs 8:12

15

PRUDENCE

All throughout history, Yahweh, the God of Abraham, Isaac and Jacob had a close relationship with His people. The first man, Adam, communed with God in the Garden of Eden. God, since the beginning, longed to communicate and interact with man whom He gave dominion over the earth. He asked Adam to name the species.

When man fell into the sin trap, the nature of man's relationship with God changed in an instant. A separation between man and God put an end to the seamless communication on a spiritual level.

Through the years, before the outpouring of the Holy Spirit, God found certain men and women that He could depend on, communicate and work with. They were men and women who proved the intent of their hearts. They sincerely loved and respected God and His ways and displayed true faith regardless of the faults and failings of their sinful nature.

Communication between God and those men and women were

not at the same level as with Adam in Eden, but still God found a way to interact with the crown of His creation. The chosen interceded on behalf of the nation or had a specific purpose to fulfill. When Jesus died on the cross, He paid the price for the sins of all men and restored the intimate relationship between God and man. Once Jesus ascended to heaven He promised that believers will never be alone, because the Holy Spirit would be sent to live in all believers who would receive Him.

The disciples, who were first to receive the Holy Spirit did great exploits and the Gospel spread like wild fire against a backdrop of persecution. Miracles followed them to prove the truth of the Gospel and God's love for all mankind. Their deeds demonstrated the dynamic Kingdom of God in action on earth.

There are many instances where the disciples describe their interaction with Holy Spirit. The miracles described in the New Testament grab most of the attention, but equally as important is that the disciples were continuously guided by the Holy Spirit.

And they went through the region of Phrygia and Galatia, having been forbidden by the Holy Spirit to speak the word in Asia. And when they had come up to Mysia, they attempted to go into Bithynia, but the Spirit of Jesus did not allow them. So, passing by Mysia, they went down to Troas. And a vision appeared to Paul in the night: a man of Macedonia was standing there, urging him and saying, "Come over to Macedonia and help us." And when Paul had seen the vision, immediately we sought to go on into Macedonia, concluding that God had called us to preach the Gospel to them.

—Acts 16:6-10

The guidance of the Holy Spirit relayed the will of the Father. It was essential to complete their assignment to preach the Gospel to all parts of the world. Through the Holy Spirit, God provided an avenue that allows for an intimate relationship with Him. An avenue that is available for those who choose to draw near. The spiritual separation between God and His people due to sin was broken once and for all through the death and resurrection of Jesus Christ.

Unfortunately we live in a world of consumer Christianity. Religious participants look to the men and women on the pulpit to provide an instant solution for their problems, instead of earnestly seeking God as individuals. Most solutions involve a process and require participation that cannot be outsourced.

God promised that the Holy Spirit would be available to dwell in all who believe, not only to appointed leaders. Although spiritual leadership is important, it should never be an excuse for believers to be passive. Individuals must foster their own relationship with God and pursue living according to Biblical principles as it is written.

A lack of spiritual application essentially leads to lives that are not robust at all. Challenges and crises invoke the default action of seeking out the wisdom of the world to find a solution. The Bible states that the wisdom of men is foolishness to God and that the Kingdom of God consists of power.

For the wisdom of this world is folly with God. For it is written, "He catches the wise in their craftiness"

—1 Corinthians 3:19

For the kingdom of God does not consist in talk but in power.

—1 Corinthians 4:20

Without the reality of an unrestrained relationship with God, some may question his/her 'religion' or believe that God is distant. They may assume that God is trapped in the Bible, with no real interest in their personal challenges.

We live in an increasingly challenging and complex world that cause many (much to Satan's delight) to believe that God is outdated. To the contrary, God has never been more instrumental in navigating our lives.

For specific choices in our everyday lives we are left with two options. Either make the decision yourself, or else inquire from the Lord and receive guidance. My journey has convinced me that the second option should always be the first stop.

THIS DUMMY's GUIDE

God created me as a practical person. I frequently ask myself the question, "How can I position myself to have a dynamic relationship with the Lord consistently?"

I know for many it may either be an irrelevant or an obvious question. I also know there are many, like me, who need some practical direction; people who need to know if a 'hand full' means three, four, five or ten peanuts. After all, not all hands are the same size!

You do not have to be in formal ministry to live a life that is pleasing to God and taps into the power and wisdom of the Creator of all things. The greatest accomplishment of Satan is to convince believers that the hope of salvation is the only inheritance of the believer in this life.

The following brief points are my personal guide (based on my journey) to draw closer to, communicate regularly with God and live a life aware of Him in every aspect. It is the principles I have identified (some the hard way) and frequently remind myself of to apply. These principles assist me to continuously grow in God and live my spiritual life effectively. Each one of us has a unique relationship with God and every individual need to determine his or her own journey. There is no quick fix but I hope that my roadmap can guide you to discover your own.

1. KNOW GOD

One's relationship with God must be grounded on the foundation of the Word. Through the Word we get to know God, understand His heart, His principles, and learn spiritual truths and Godly wisdom.

The Bible is clear about God's expectations on how to conduct our lives, how to treat others and how to serve and worship Him. The Word is the sword of the Spirit, the weapon with which we defeat Satan and our flesh. You cannot effectively use this sword if you don't know what it is made of or how to handle it.

...and take the helmet of salvation, and the sword of the Spirit, which is the word of God

—Ephesians 6:17-18

One of the most frequent ways that God communicates with me is simply through His Word. He typically leads me to specific passages (often I see it in my mind), that apply to my situation when I need wisdom on a particular day. I don't always get this direction from God, but when I do it is ninety percent applicable. Why do I specifically state ninety percent? Because I am committed to the truth, and the truth is that no one gets it right all the time. Confirmation is a good principle to apply at all times.

The Lord desires that we engage with Him and the Bible states that we need to pray without ceasing. A lot of people dread prayer, thinking that it is boring and they do not know what to say. Prayer is only boring if you don't expect a response or if you recite a religious poem with no real meaning. It is ineffective when you feel you cannot share the ugly, the painful and the hilariously funny things with God. Maybe you have been told it is not appropriate.

My best prayer sessions with God were when I had a real 'hard truth' conversation with the Lord. On those occasions my heart was filled with passion stemming from pain, guilt, anger or pure joy.

God is majestic and we should treat Him in this manner, but it does not mean we cannot be ourselves. God is holy and we need to approach Him in the right way. That means entering into His presence with awe and reverence. Greet Him with worship, praise and thanksgiving. Ask for forgiveness and seek His direction.

Once God has been honored in this way, we can approach Him in the name of Jesus. We can stand boldly before Him and engage with a God that listens and understands.

For we do not have a high priest who is unable to sympathize with our weaknesses, but one who in every respect has been tempted as we are, yet without sin. Let us then with confidence draw near to the throne of grace, that we may receive mercy and find grace to help in time of need.

—Hebrews 4:15-16

Listen to what God speaks to your heart or contemplate the scripture you have read and see if the Lord reveals an application to your life.

I learned the hard way that spending time with God must be one's first priority. If you put Him first, He will take care of the rest. More importantly, He will remain close. God understands a busy day or even a busy season in your life, but the spiritual principle remain clear; "seek first the Kingdom of God and all things will be given to you."

God will communicate even when you are in a rush depending on the level of intimacy in your relationship with Him.

2. REPENT

Sin which stems from disobedience to God's Word and teachings, I believe, is the most common reason why Christians experience dead religion instead of an interactive relationship. The Bible is clear that there is no blessing where sin prevails.

> Do not be deceived: God is not mocked, for whatever one sows, that will he also reap. For the one who sows to his own flesh will from the flesh reap corruption, but the one who sows to the Spirit will from the Spirit reap eternal life.
>
> —Galatians 6:7-8

Mankind is expected to live a righteous life in obedience to God. We all sin and have fallen short of the measure that God put in place. God knows the intent of hearts and both God and Satan observe our actions in public *and* in private.

Hearing and interacting with God is a blessing and a privilege in itself. We cannot expect God to answer our prayers and communicate with us if we live in habitual sin or harbor resentment. It is not possible to live a sinless life, but it is certainly possible to intentionally avoid opportunity to sin. With the Holy Spirit as our counselor and conscience we can overcome the flesh with His power.

Typically it is a simple case of what you desire most. To know and please God and experience His blessings or to indulge in the short-lived pleasurers of sin.

Talk is cheap. One has to walk the walk. Living according to God's Word protects us from the accusations from Satan. It reduces Satan's opportunity to attack us if we do not give him anything to work with.

I can testify from my personal experience that God withdraws when we persist in any habitual sin (in accordance with His Word). He will engage to warn and point us back to the right path but will eventually turn completely silent if we persist. Holiness and evil do not mix.

The Bible states that when we repent, He will remove our sins from us, as far as the east is from the west! Satan cannot use it against us anymore. That is the Good News of the Gospel.

As I got to know the Lord and built a relationship with the Father, it became apparent just how important it is to live according to His Word and to be obedient. It is a process and God knows that. He will help you. He knows whether you are sincere in your efforts or not. If you are, you will find that your efforts will bear fruit.

God is good and wants the best for us. He wants us to succeed. He feels our hurt when we open ourselves up to the attacks of Satan.

Repentance practically means to ask for forgiveness, stop what you have been doing, saying or thinking and apply more of God's Word in your life. Beware, you cannot bribe or fool God. If you give your tithe, go to church, and do good but your private life is full of willful disobedience, you will experience separation from God.

Renew your mind, fill your heart with expectation and your actions should follow. I am far from perfect and it took some time to overcome a few strongholds in my life, but by giving it my all, God was never silent. At times when I tried to make my sin 'acceptable' God was silent.

3. ASK

Ask, and it shall be given you; seek, and ye shall find; knock, and it shall be opened unto you

—Matthew 7:7

The Bible teaches that God already knows what we need before we even ask for it. He is ready to provide for our needs. Yet in Matthew 7 believers are instructed to ask, seek and knock or pursue.

As believers we must ask in confidence and with faith in expectation of a response. It is important not to frame your request within what you believe is possible by natural means alone. Quite often God's response and intervention works outside the limit we place on possible solutions.

We live in a time where 'normal' solutions will not be enough to enforce the truth, and bring light into our personal lives and into the world. Understand the dynamic truth that life and death is in

185

the power of the tongue. All of creation exists through the words that God spoke in the beginning – "There shall be..." There is power both in communicating dependence on God and declaring our intent to all creation; both the natural and spiritual.

I suggest proposing a personal protocol (sign) to the Lord to communicate His presence in your life and to confirm His guidance. This typically would be something that has meaning to you. For me it is the number *seven* specifically but also other numbers as described in earlier chapters. It does not mean that God will always use this method of communication. It also does not mean that you cannot request a different method as your relationship progresses and life circumstances change. I was amazed how much the Lord is willing to engage with a sincere heart in a way that resonates with my individual personality.

A detailed God shows His splendor in the detail. Doubt often threatens to convince us that we have no right to expect such a close relationship with God. Doubt is correct, we don't have a right; we are privileged to approach God in the name of Jesus Christ who paid a high price for our access to the Father. That is how much God loves and desires an intimate relationship with His people.

4. BE ALERT

Once you have communicated your request and possibly established a protocol with God, both immediate expectation and patience is required.

The Lord may speak immediately or it may take a while. Normal prayer time and communing with God should be maintained. Prayer is often considered as a once-off event, especially in stressful times. If we presume that nothing is happening, we simply give up and accept there is no help. In my encounters this was a huge mistake!

God answers in wisdom, guidance or miracles. His guidance can include a multiphase plan or process. It may include making adjustments along the way to receive the fullness of what God has in store.

Another possibility is that opposing forces are trying to prevent you from receiving a response either in the form of God speaking to you or a breakthrough that is required. Recently, I waited for more than a month to see the Lord provide the breakthrough which He had communicated in the first few days. I did not understand why the specific request took so long. At the end the Lord clearly communicated a passage from Daniel. Daniel had to wait three weeks for a response from God because of the spiritual principality that opposed the angel. Even though I did not have to wait for communication, I did have to wait more than a month to see the manifestation of God's communication.

Often in times like this we start to doubt that we actually heard from the Lord and even start to question well established truths in our lives. At times when a response from God does not fit our paradigm it is often ignored.

If the response does not make sense, ask for clarification. Ask if there are any intermediate steps or actions that the Lord wants you to take. God will reconfirm His answer in the midst of a battle. Most importantly stay alert!

Areas where I expect the Lord to communicate to me are:

- Scripture. Either through daily study or presented by the Holy Spirit (in my spirit or my mind).
- Speaking to my heart in a still small voice.

- My agreed protocol with the Lord. This could be presented anywhere – in a magazine, on a bank statement, on the side of a truck or a plane, on a leaflet, through words spoken, in the news, in the properties of a computer file, in the dimensions of a design, in a book, in a movie, projected on a screen during a meeting both secular or church related, the gate number of the flight that I am boarding, a time stamp – anything is possible.

- Sermons

- Devotions

- A person communicating a message directly related to the request without them knowing about it at all. This could be either a believer or a secular person.

- Nature

- Dreams. I never expected the Lord to speak to me through dreams. I was not the dream guy. My sister-in-law however introduced me to teachings and guidance on how to interpret our dreams. Once I started analyzing any noteworthy (strange) dreams it was clear that God still communicates through dreams and to a normal person like me. Recently I revisited a dream I had three years ago and it was incredible how accurately it foretold the past three years in my life. In many ways it acted as encouragement to persevere.

- Visions. Since I started writing this book I experienced two visions in the early morning hours. Again this was not a method of communication from the Lord that I thought was a spiritual gift of mine, but it happened. It was required at the time and God reached out dynamically. The visions were intense and I believe critically important revelations to assist me in my personal spiritual development.

Do not disqualify yourself from any method of communication from the Lord. It is crucial for believers in the Kingdom of God to operate in power to fulfill God's purposes on earth. There are some powerful people in the secular world that made several deals with the occult to achieve their goals. It is essential to exercise your privilege as a child of God to walk in the power of the Holy Spirit, guided by Jesus Christ and with the authority of the Father.

I have to present a brief warning. Always seek the truth and scrutinize any spiritual experience that you have. God is not mocked and any *intentional* 'self-manufactured' engagement with God used for self-interest will not end without consequences. This is true especially when your actions affect others.

5. SEEK CONFIRMATION

Apply the Gideon principle and seek confirmation. As a rule my wife and I always request three confirmations when we receive instruction that is life changing or could have a major impact on another person.

This principle has served us well to confirm that we are indeed hearing from the Lord and not our own will. Moving countries for the second time, the Lord provided the same confirmation three times. We needed the assurance to persist.

Seeking confirmation requires patience but serves to provide the confidence that is required to move forward in power and to sustain the effort.

~~~~~~

One of our American friends applied this principle upon planning a return trip to South Africa. She asked the Lord if He would use her to do something relevant for Him. One evening she felt like looking at the airfares to South Africa to get an idea of current prices. Two weeks prior, my brother contacted me to inquire if our friend would be interested to serve at a camp for orphans that they were hosting. I was sure that she would consider it and if they needed more hands we knew some other parties that could be interested too. My brother however explained that he specifically heard our friend's name from the Lord, so I provided her phone number and e-mail.

Several days later he decided to phone our friend and as the Lord planned it, it happen to be the day after she looked at flights and asked the Lord to use her. When she received the phone call, she just said "yes" not even knowing exactly what for, because she knew it was the Lord.

Three confirmations for her included for the first time in years being free from coaching softball, having the desire to travel to South Africa and the timing in receiving the phone call. God answered, and because she was alert, she could identify the Lord's communication. Needless to say, the trip turned out to be very special for her and those she served.

~~~~~~~

On some occasions God answers so clearly that confirmation is not required and asking for it would be an attempt to avoid acting on the Lord's command. It may sound like I am contradicting myself. Let me explain.

A more challenging moment for me was when I felt the

presence of an oppressing spirit in the office. I believed that it was attached to specific ornaments. One of the ornaments resided in my office. Since its presence in my office, I had outbursts of anger over the phone and a real somber mood beset my space. After thinking and praying about it overnight, I decided to place the ornament outside my office for the duration of a possibly contentious teleconference first thing in the morning.

The teleconference went really well and afterward I decided to take the ornament and do a prayer-walk outside the building 'cleaning' it from any entities that were attached to it. It required fervent prayer and I experienced resistance but it worked and peace was restored in my office.

My manager at the time did have a Christian background, but I would not describe him as a born-again Christian. Even though he was a pragmatic person, broaching the subject and telling him that I plan to pray over his office and all the other cubicles, would probably register on his 'insane' scale.

I felt a strong presence of the Lord during an informal discussion with my manager, when he explained that everything seemed to be going wrong and normal everyday activities would get under his skin. The still small voice inside me was saying that I should talk to him about the ornaments and their influence. I should also pray over the whole section that was afflicted in the office.

This would definitely fall into the category of a career limiting move but God did not leave me alone. I asked Him for confirmation that I was not imagining things. If He would give me clear direction that I was not losing my mind, I would be obedient.

The Lord did not waste any time. I was making my way back to office after lunch and decided to read my daily devotion. I opened up the web page and the "verse for the day" jumped out from the page,

> And whenever those possessed by evil spirits caught sight of him, the spirits would throw them to the ground in front of him shrieking, 'You are the Son of God!'"
>
> —Mark 3:11

I did not need any further confirmation. This was not a typical verse for the day and it was directly related to what I believed we faced.

I took my manager for lunch the next day. I explained what I believed was the source of the unusual behaviors and that I would pray over the office. During the conversation, he mentioned that some of his personnel were having trouble sleeping and were stressed out over trivial matters.

The Lord prepared the ground and I was obedient. In this case, asking for additional confirmation would be delayed obedience with the intention to save myself embarrassment. It would have been an attempt to shy away from acknowledging the Name and the Power of the Lord Jesus Christ in front of others.

6. ACT AND ACKNOWLEDGE

The only way to learn to effectively communicate with the Lord, and to consistently discern between thoughts or ideas and the voice of the Lord, is by acting. Not all communication from the Lord involves acting. Sometimes His communication announces His presence or brings comfort. Any communication that includes instruction or guidance implies that you should act. Often acting involves a churning stomach and overcoming fear to move forward. Because of fear a multitude of believers never or only by exception, act on communication from the Lord. This often is the case when believers try to take shortcuts in their relationship with the Lord. God describes those He has a relationship with as friends, not acquaintances.

Hearing the voice of the Lord has no value if it does not translate into action that impact your own life, your family's life, another's life or society in general. Practically, the only way you will ever know for sure if your communication channel with the Lord is functioning is by acting on His message or more specifically, by taking risk.

God does not expect us to take huge risks from the start and we shouldn't. He is a loving God and leads us through His grace and mercy from faith for faith. His desire is a continuous progression as we grow in our relationship with Him.

> For in it the righteousness of God is revealed from faith for faith, as it is written, 'The righteous shall live by faith.'
>
> —Romans 1:17

The best place to start? Listen to God's voice regarding the adjustments He wants you to make in your life and that of your family. Be responsive to the areas that need to be (more) aligned with His Word.

You should soon notice the positive impact of communicating with God and applying His direction. Be alert to God's communication in the personal decisions that you have to make at home and also in the workplace. Ask him to help you with everyday tasks and engagements and act on His guidance.

Inquire from the Lord for any major life changing decisions and once you have received sufficient confirmation move ahead and be obedient to the Lord's communication and trust Him.

7. PERSEVERE

Our God is a good God. It is important to always approach and interpret circumstances from this point of view. The Bible is full of the blessings that God has in store for those who believe. The biggest blessing of all is to be called a child of God.

Once you endeavor to make God an integral part of your life and engage in a deeper, more powerful relationship with Him, you will probably appear on the enemy's radar. Satan is quite content for us to wander around his territory keeping to ourselves, living a good life. This typically changes when you live the principles of the Bible, including the 'unpopular' ones. We are seen as a real threat as soon as we start to operate in the power of the Kingdom and work with God in a dynamic way.

You will probably face opposition when God's Spirit lead and empower you to break down Satan's strongholds and deviate from society's set norms. Opposition, setbacks and mistakes will cause doubt in your mind. Some facts might testify against what the Lord communicated to you. Perseverance is required and tangibly demonstrates our faith and release the power of God and His angels.

Perseverance means to continue to praise, thank and honor God that He is fighting the battle on your behalf in the spiritual realm. Naturally it means to speak and think as per the communication received from the Lord. When you experience a moment of despair, put a guard in front of your mouth. Say nothing if it is not in agreement of what the Lord communicated. Continue to work at what the Lord instructed and maintain a long term view.

Speak to the Lord and ask Him to bless you by leaving His 'calling card' along the road. It doesn't matter how difficult the circumstances, every time that the Lord confirms His involvement, I experience peace and hope.

Yoked with the unstoppable force of the Creator, one should always be alert for any assistance from God. I experienced a significant spiritual attack once but God warned me beforehand in a spectacular way. I was waiting in a room when the normal music on the speakers was interrupted by interference from a police radio. The officer said that a whirlwind had touched down on a road very close to our house. I could not make out the rest and the interference stopped after a minute or so. Only a few days later equipment that I use failed at critical times for no reason, and had a big impact on my new venture. I remembered the whirlwind which can be a sign of spiritual danger (including witchcraft) in the Bible, and acted accordingly in prayer. God went to great lengths that time to communicate the danger – for good reason. Knowing what was happening gave me the determination and knowledge I needed to persevere.

The complete cycle of inquiring, hearing, acting and achieving may take minutes, hours, days, months or years. It depends on the nature of assignment. In my experience nothing of lasting value or impact happens without perseverance.

An attempt to persevere by oneself and to carry the burden as an individual, typically leads to burnout. Always stay in touch with God and work as part of His team, not an independent contractor. Seek counselling and support from peers, gather prayer support, develop your spiritual skills through informal education and commune with likeminded people.

Living the journey with God takes us into the Promised Land. A place occupied by giants and nations stronger than us, but also a land where the battle is the Lord's and fulfillment is abundant.

John answered and said, A man can receive nothing, except it be given him from heaven.

—John 3:27

16

PROCESS

I just couldn't keep the engineer inside of me locked up in his cage. I had to summarize my approach through a functional delineation for easy reference.

The execution of projects involves several phases, each phase with its own steps to completion. Alongside the project execution methodology, quality control and validation or verification activities monitor and control the execution of the project. These activities help team members to complete their work according to policies and procedures required by the customer. It confirms that what is designed or planned is in line with what the customer wants and that the solution which is finally implemented meets the requirements. This in turn ensures that at delivery time, the end product is acceptable to the customer and fulfills the intended purpose.

During the project life cycle, designs and implementation modules are reviewed or tested and reworked if required. In more complex projects information from the customer is received in phases and as required to progress.

From my perspective, a similar process can be applied when we are dynamically engaging with God. By remaining in continuous communication with the Lord we can ensure that we proceed according to His will, receive information from Him when required and test our thoughts and ideas.

Close collaboration with God changes our perspective. Opposition, setbacks and mistakes result in adjustments and improvement rather than termination. With the completion of each cycle with God, we are better equipped. Quitting when facing setbacks or seemingly insurmountable odds keeps us just where the enemy wants us, imprisoned by our own natural abilities.

The flow diagram included in this chapter serves as a reminder to me of the lessons that I learned on my journey. It helps me to manage my relationship with God in an efficient way. Execution is subject to God's approval and sovereign veto right! I pray that it would be a blessing to you too.

PROCESS

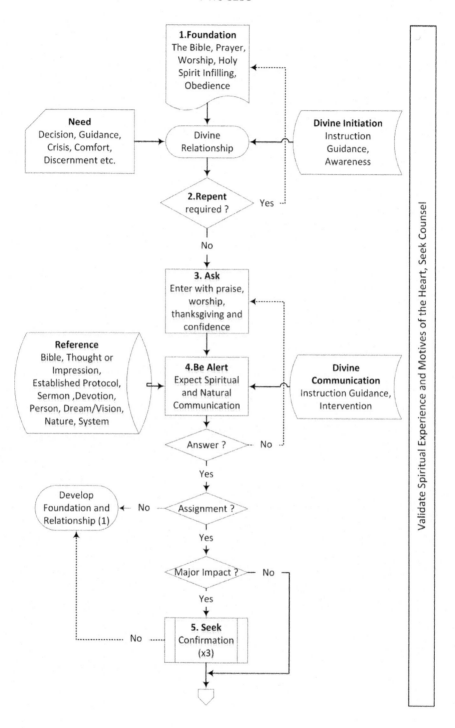

201

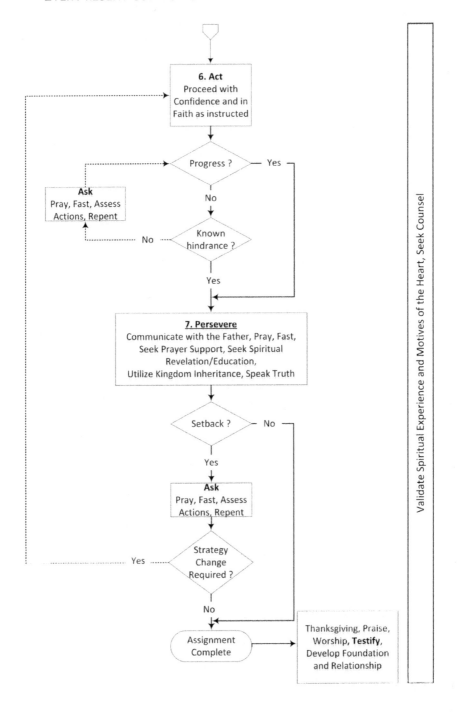

"…But, as it is written, What no eye has seen, nor ear heard, nor the heart of man imagined, what God has prepared for those who love him"— these things God has revealed to us through the Spirit. For the Spirit searches everything, even the depths of God.

—2 Corinthians 9-10

17

LIVE IN THE SPIRIT

I believe that the not too distant future will require more than human wisdom and strength to navigate. Mankind will not be able to depend on their culture for moral guidance.

Satan knows the best way to destroy the enemy (the Church) is from within. Mainstream culture in the West has largely retained a form of Christianity that lacks spiritual authority. Human wisdom pollutes the truth and strips the Word of God from its power. Religion without the Spirit of God fails to provide discernment, invoke change and deliver practitioners from strongholds in their lives.

Another clever technique that Satan uses is to counterfeit what God designed for good, to bring doubt, disbelief and distortion into the church. Some have shunned the gifts of the Holy Spirit because of counterfeit shepherds and churches that manufacture spiritual encounters.

In both instances, the result is the same - believers that do not live in the Spirit.

> But understand this, that in the last days there will come times of
> difficulty. For people will be lovers of self, lovers of money, proud,
> arrogant, abusive, disobedient to their parents, ungrateful, unholy,
> heartless, unappeasable, slanderous, without self-control, brutal,
> not loving good, treacherous, reckless, swollen with conceit, lovers
> of pleasure rather than lovers of God, having the appearance of
> godliness, but denying its power. Avoid such people.
> —2 Timothy 1:1-5 (Emphasis added)

God called His followers to live according to the Spirit and
accept our identity as heirs in the Kingdom of God. We must be
determined to establish ourselves spiritually and find an
environment of like-minded people that are committed to the truth.

> So then, brothers, we are debtors, not to the flesh, to live according
> to the flesh. For if you live according to the flesh you will die, but
> if by the Spirit you put to death the deeds of the body, you will live.
> For all who are led by the Spirit of God are sons of God. For you
> did not receive the spirit of slavery to fall back into fear, but you
> have received the Spirit of adoption as sons, by whom we cry,
> Abba! Father!" The Spirit himself bears witness with our spirit that
> we are children of God, and if children, then heirs—heirs of God
> and fellow heirs with Christ, provided we suffer with him in order
> that we may also be glorified with him.
> —Romans 8:12-17

True believers will have to be prepared and aware. We will have
to continuously depend on the Holy Spirit to discern between truth
and deception. Do not miss out on the fullness of a Spirit-filled

relationship with God because of the failures of man and the cunningness of evil. Take ownership of your relationship with God. Identify any bad experiences for what they are, learn from them and start fresh. Do not let your inheritance go to waste. The Bible contains precious truth, that together with the Holy Spirit, allows us to overcome in His power if we can harness the fullness of our identity in Christ.

Spiritual growth is not possible without putting in the effort. Stay focused and be determined to succeed in growing closer to God. I pray that you will be blessed with a real, dynamic and intimate relationship.

The greatest football fan may know all the rules of the game, what the role is of each player and even if they are performing their function well. The fan would however be destroyed if he attempts to play as a professional without ever having played the game at a lower level or even in his back yard.

Knowing the path and walking the path is not the same. If you choose to pursue a more dynamic relationship with God, I suggest that you start small. Begin your journey with God by taking risks in a safe and forgiving environment. Allow yourself the space to grow. God will honor that and lead you with His instruction.

I find it useful to keep a journal detailing the instances when God communicated. I include information on when, how and the action that resulted from the communication as well as the outcome. This is a useful tool to strengthen one's faith when you face future challenges and also to learn from one's mistakes.

Only when you are confident that you are able to observe and discern God's guidance in your personal space is it time to venture out. Do not short circuit the process. Build a solid foundation and confidence first. If you choose to share a word of knowledge with a friend, a fellow church member, a colleague or even a stranger, always proceed with humility.

Through my journey that I have shared in this book, I pray that you will know that God is all-powerful, ever present and available. There is no situation or circumstance out of His reach and He wants to walk with you on your journey, bringing glory to the Kingdom of God. The Father is evident in the details and created you the way you are. His door is open to all who seek Him and He will engage with you in a way that resonates with your character.

The Father's intent towards man has not changed. God is alive and is actively searching the earth for men and women to call upon, not only to be missionaries in a foreign land but also to raise a monument to His name in all areas of life. Men and women that will testify of the grace, love, majesty, might and glory of God in every forum. People that do not merely stand, but excel in the name of righteousness.

God is looking for shepherds that lead from the front by example and not merely with words that have not manifested in their own lives. He is looking for parents that raise their children by example in a home that is saturated with the presence of the Holy Spirit. The Father is searching for young adults that honor their parents and channel their energy and vigor in service of His Kingdom.

The most exciting times in the history of mankind is approaching and Jesus is looking for His followers to be champions.

He shall seduce with flattery those who violate the covenant, but the people who know their God shall stand firm and take action.

—Daniel 11:32

Our strength is in the power of the Holy Spirit that works through us. His ability is without equal. It is only logical that developing a personal dynamic relationship with God should be the priority above all else.

I challenge you to make a choice, humble yourself, believe and live in the Spirit. This analytical engineer did and never looked back.

ABOUT THE AUTHOR

Casper J. van Tonder

Casper worked as an automation, control and safety systems engineer for sixteen years, primarily in the oil and gas industry. During this time he was involved as Lead Engineer on mega projects for global customers and worked in many countries and with many cultures.

Casper attributes his success to God's grace and mercy in his life. His experience led him to become the Americas Engineering Excellence Leader for his company before he felt that God called him to pursue a different assignment.

Casper lived in several countries including South Africa, Republic of Ireland, United Kingdom and United States of America. He volunteered as youth pastor and teaching pastor over the years. His faith is a priority in his life. Casper and his wife Vita lives in Houston Texas at the time of printing.

Visit the author's web page: caspervantonder.com

CPSIA information can be obtained at www.ICGtesting.com
Printed in the USA
LVOW04s0702231214

420093LV00007B/82/P